AMERICAN DARKNESS

A POETIC JOURNEY WITH SHORT STORIES THAT TREK THROUGH DARKNESS TO FIND THE LIGHT

AMERICAN DARKNESS

A POETIC JOURNEY WITH SHORT STORIES THAT TREK THROUGH DARKNESS TO FIND THE LIGHT

STEVEN SKIBICKI

Fresh Ink Group
Guntersville

American Darkness

Fresh Ink Group
An Imprint of:
The Fresh Ink Group, LLC
1021 Blount Avenue #931
Guntersville, AL 35976
Email: info@FreshInkGroup.com
FreshInkGroup.com

Edition 1.0 2023

Cover design by Stephen Geez / FIG
Book design by Amit Dey / FIG
Associate publisher Beem Weeks / FIG

Cataloging-in-Publication Recommendations:
POE023010 **POETRY** / Subjects & Themes / Death, Grief, Loss
POE005010 POETRY / American / General
FIC082000 **FICTION** / Own Voices

Library of Congress Control Number: 2023921952

ISBN-13: 978-1-958922-01-9 Papercover
ISBN-13: 978-1-958922-02-6 Hardcover
ISBN-13: 978-1-958922-03-3 Ebooks

Table of Contents

Epigraph

"Life isn't just about darkness or light, rather it's about finding light within the darkness."

— Landon Parham, author of first summer of night.

"What makes night within us may leave stars."

— Victor Hugo, author of *Cimourdain*

"Not till we are lost, in other words not till we have lost the world, do we begin to find ourselves, and realize where we are and the infinite extent of our relations"

— Henry David Thoreau, author of Walden

"Just because no one else can heal or do your inner work for you doesn't mean you can, should, or need to do it alone."

— Lisa Olivera, author and therapist

"My dark days made me strong. Or maybe I already was strong, and they made me prove it."

— Emery Lord, author of when we collided

"You don't have to be positive all the time. It's perfectly okay to feel sad, angry, annoyed, frustrated, scared and anxious. Having feelings doesn't make you a negative person. It makes you human."

— Lori Deschene, author of the tiny Buddha series

"Mental health problems don't define who you are. They are something you experience. You walk in the rain and you feel the rain, but you are not the rain."

— Matt Haig, author.

"The most beautiful people we have known are those who have known defeat, known suffering, known struggle, known loss, and have found their way out of the depths. These persons have an appreciation, a sensitivity, and an understanding of life that fills them with compassion, gentleness, and a deep loving concern. Beautiful people do not just happen."

— Elisabeth Kübler-Ross, author and psychiatrist

An explanation before the journey

Inside, beyond these pages lies a book of poetry, poetry that started at a very early age learning to cope with mental illness that hadn't been diagnosed yet and the bad things that happened. As a result of life mixing into a swirl of misery atop a sundae of bad happenstance, I was an angry child, I got into fights often. I was abused to put it bluntly; my father was a coke addict and my mother worked two jobs just to make things come together. On top of that I was poor, many of the things I enjoyed were handed down to me and so at the age of twelve I picked up writing as a means to cope at the suggestion of an English teacher from Kearsarge regional middle school in New Hampshire.

For years I wrote, and I wrote putting both my heart and soul down onto a page that sometimes-other people would read and sometimes they would roll their eyes and say, "hey just publish a book already." I dealt with many people who had the audacity to ask why I was writing the kind of stuff that I was writing, "it's pretty dark," but it's in the darkness that I found the light. It did not take very long for me to realize that the more I wrote, the better I felt, and I turned that pain and sadness into art that other people read, that they actually enjoyed. They felt like they had gotten an insight, or they could relate and say that they never had the words to be able to describe something that they were going through at the time. Some part of me would still like to ask why I didn't come and do this sooner, well sometimes life gets in the way; other times we doubt ourselves and it falls into hindsight.

Hindsight is a 20/20 insight to all of the things you should have done differently and some things you did accomplish correctly. This book is something I hope that I accomplished correctly, not for critical acclaim or fifteen minutes of fame but to serve as a reminder to other people that no matter what they happen to be going through that they are not alone. This book and I hope to help people that are looking into the darkness, and they feel like it's staring back into them. So that if they need to, they can pop it open and understand that someone else understands, it may not be the exact piece of the abyss that they happen to be staring into. That is just it though, while it may seem different, and that we are staring into two entirely different black pits that look like they are going to swallow us whole.

The reality of it is that darkness is rarely separate from one another; people may argue that a shadow is different from the blackness of space, but I say that it's not a contest and it all exists in the same spectrum. Now before this piece of literature commences, I'd like to take a moment to talk to you the reader (yes you) beyond my own personal story and why I'm doing what I'm doing by publishing this book. You are not your sadness, you are not your mental illness, you are you and any stigma anyone has placed on you for going through what you're going through as a result of genetics or something terrible that happened. You will always be better than that, you are a warrior; you can conquer and push this thing back to where it belongs as just a part of you. You can even turn it into art or whatever it is that your heart wishes to pursue, you will forever be more than the circumstances that happened to hit your life.

If you've taken the time to read this, I greatly appreciate it and hope you take up what I just had to say to your heart for the journey you happen to be on and find peace. Oh right, the wall of quotes in the epigraph, that is so you know that you're not alone; that there really are a lot of us out here reaching back for the ones still staring at the darkness. Because we have seen it as well, and we know the kind of pull it has to it. After all it's not just me reaching down for you or anyone you may know, even if right now you're just reading because you like dark themes. Should you find yourself there, we are here for you too.

The manic-depressive mind

The mountains and the depths of the ocean define my days,
I climb so high that I and Icarus can see the wings upon each other.
For a temporal moment, I am there blinded by the ebullient radiation,
until I begin to plunge downwards to the shimmering waters cover.

Then on my descent to the epitome of darkened despair,
I release my hope as I wave to the sunken metropolis of Atlantis.
Just as I feel my soul slide down to die, I am filled with searing air,
rage and angst start to drag me back up to the surface.

Caught in a blatant, frantic struggle against my own emotion,
I go forth meticulously in a never-ending brawl against myself.
With it forcing me to mountainous highs and to the depths of the ocean,
who could bear to be close to one who is at war with themselves?

For day in and day out either raised way up to the state of mania,
or to be sunken below in depression debating the loss of their sanity

Cherry blossom

Cherry blossom how I wish I could blush like you,
so that when the flavor of my life were to kiss me,
Even if for a brief moment I could show my heart's truth,
so that I may not be further shackled by pride but be free.

Cherry blossom if you only knew my jealousy of your rouge,
yet somehow still I can't help but gawk at your pure beauty.
You have nothing to do with this game of love, and how I lose,
nor do you have the power to take my pride tied together with idiocy.

However, cherry blossom, oh cherry blossom, you still drive me envious,
I need your rouge so that I may show my hearts only fervent desire.
Even if it were to grant the illusion to me that I was beyond deciduous,
as long as my cherry blossom knew she was my passion's fire.

I could believe in the river of my soul that my job was done,
that my cherry blossom knew she was planted by that river under the sun.

Wrath

Veins bursting, and blood coursing to shoot out like Mount Vesuvius.
Bind me if you dare to take the imposing old dance with the lady of fate.
If you come to bar me, I'll be the atom bomb and you can be Hiroshima,
capitulate to your maleficent overcomer, just lay down to become sedated.

Your strength alone, cannot place me back inside of my battered cage,
strike me left, strike me right, disintegrate my bones in your sight.
The open sepulcher will spew forth, driving me on inside of my rage.
a whole room will feel as if it were a blazing inferno on a subarctic night.

I am beyond bane, vipers could not even ensnare me with their blight,
I incite immorality with my hushed whispers in the ears of all who fall prey.
Do not emblazon yourself by quarreling against me on this igneous night.
we know who you run to when the candle burns down, and the wick frays.

Go ahead you charlatan, cast me aside as you walk your life's path,
I know you shall eventually return to lay your claim upon more wrath.

Greed

Gaining the entire world won't allow you to emerge insidiously,
go ahead my salacious friend, what's to Mar if you take it all?
If you're exposed in supernal light your pneuma won't appear hideous,
it's a day before the harvest, so you've got time before you fall.

Can't even touch you kid if you line yourself with lucre like myself,
the entirety of the sphere will wish upon a star to be in your likeness.
So sling on a simper, baptize yourself in gold with all of this wealth,
only exist once, surely it won't incapacitate you to be rife with selfishness.

Pivot your nose upward to that beggar in need of your assistance,
layer yourself in all the articles of this globe until you omit your soul.
Clutch my hand you incautious friend have faith in my insistence,
come now, if the sovereigns of old were here, they'd worship your soles.

I know that you have grown old, but the black robe isn't a servant for hire,
ecstatic you've listened to every word, now I'll have a new friend in the fire.

Gluttony

Eat, drink, and be merry for on the morrow's eve we die,
eat until your heart is filled with illustrious beatific illumination.
To consume is good for your health, so just let out a relieved sigh,
it's not as if an extra pound or two will ultimately lead you to damnation.

Moderation is for simpletons who don't sense enough to enjoy life,
they remain blissfully incognizant of what it is to be the life of the party.
Ignore your loved ones, they will never decipher, they're caught in strife,
how could they apprehend how it fills you with joy to devour so heartily.

What's a pygmy kidney failure, cirrhosis, artery calcification, or stroke,
don't unchain your idols now, you have sufficient time to repent.
Plaster that inner temple of yours with fare until the altar is broke,
ravage and attain your temporal desires until you have waxed spent.

I say these enamoring words, so in all truth it is quite a funny thing,
despite my intentions, they haven't realized they're puppets on my string.

Pride

I shall ascend above all of those in the mount of the congregation,
for they are all subservient to the quintessence residing in my form.
The architect of the undivided universe will bow before me in subjugation,
those wretched mortals will be cleansed and my layout will be the norm.

I shall tread and summon forth my sword with one-third of the host,
how could I possibly lose with such a great impetus against the incumbent?
My military shall avenge my lacerations, endowing only me to boast,
blood may fall down to traverse the heavens but I can remain enchanted.

What is this? How could I lose, I was the alpha, I was the paradigm
for which all creation was made after, how dare they obliterate my beauty.
Despite my wings incineration, I will rise and seek justice for this crime,
before my time elapses you will feel my fist and your own futility.

Since I couldn't assume my rightful place since the very beginning,
listen here god knows the day you eat of this fruit you will be like him.

Sloth

Do not fret, they will find a way to resolve this amongst themselves,
they're all ingenious, it's not as if you have that type of approbation.
The dust on the bottom of my boots contain substantially more wealth,
the air you breathe costs more than your effort, just go back to sedation.

Your hands being idle is greater than any pitiful effort you could produce,
just sit back, and watch the events go by, what difference could you make?
Want to change things? Go ahead if you want to be the subject of abuse,
I mean what else could you possibly be? You behemoth of a mistake.

I'm euphoric, you decided to accept the only thing that makes sense,
that you're a walking oversight, a lumbering tower of uselessness.
Just go lay yourself down to be inoperative, listen to your conscience,
life is a game and it's wise if you stay immobilized in this chaotic mess.

My drowsy-eyed, utterly defeated friend, you want to know my name?
I am the destroyer of all hope and action, I am the author of your demise.
I made you unable to function until you were inept to make a change,
I worked you over the coals until I became your damnation in disguise.

Envy

The grass is always greener over on the other side of the fence,
the atmosphere is always more azure from someone else's view.
It's not a fallacy to dream, what is so imposing of your covetousness?
Theft may be a sin but nothing is lost in setting your eyes on something new.

The lord of hosts cares not if what you seek belongs to another,
not as if you are taking a prized possession and lifting it from his grasp.
After all, in this new age, that old testament has no power, my brother,
no need for any more trembling of consequences, just sit back and relax.

Now just meander for a few more brief moments in relation to me,
give up and give in to the relentless urge to have the materials of others.
Do it for spite, for malice, relentlessly pursue until you're too blind to see,
chase it down with the rigid pit in your stomach continuously seething.

Keep me in the back of your mind like when you first sat in fear and awe,
that it was always me cutting you off from grace like a broken tooth saw.

My nightmare

Waking drenched in sweat with a rush to cleanse, and urge to purge,
rapidly hot with no cold water churning in with the faucets hum.
Scouring already clean hands, that to many others have been a scourge,
a man peers into the reflection of an abysmal mirror feeling like scum.

As water courses over the calloused digits, the night terror resumes,
with vivid apparitions returning to torment the already afflicted.
The evisceration of the soul makes his heart feel like lying down in a tomb,
there never appeared to be a medicament for that visionary sickness.

Rigorous shame pierced a heart adulterated with elevated abhorrence,
razors couldn't scrape away, a faucet with its inability to lave the stains
upon the fists.
Tears couldn't lessen their effect as that sinner's celestial penance,
any effort leads to more suffering to remain ultimately in subsistence.

Perdition was realized in the mortal realm recorded in times ethereal sands,
manifesting in the vile form of blood never to be cleansed from the hands.

The greatest of these

Given everything to charities of the sphere until you've gone broke,
but where is that tender bleeding heart filled with endearment?
Have you been taught nothing about the axis upon which we rotate,
if you do everything in your power but do not love, you have reason to fear.

That you have just gone completely bankrupt in the depths of your soul,
people can say the greatest enamoring speech in the history of the earth.
Yet if they do not feel the sparks themselves they are just a clanging cymbal,
if they don't come under it as well they are just hot smoke soon to disperse.

If they were to go to the stake to burn as the grandest martyr,
yet not outwardly show the deepness of their affection they've gone in vain.
Instill the greatest wisdom in the young, yet not love, they're a common cur,
to do everything in the world, yet not give the gift of love is just insane.

For it is long written down as the vastest commandment from above,
that among all of these things the most crucial is to love.

The tongue

Watch your tongue lad, you've got no idea the power inside of your lips,
It can be the paintbrush that strokes amber rays on new beginnings.
Yet even so, it can transform into a megaton bomb only you can equip.
The words work to make an epic tale or a dreadfully abysmal ending.

Chain it up and catapult away the key if you must to save their lives,
for you are blissfully ignorant of the bane allocated in there.
It's the power to burn them to cinders with flames flickering insidiously,
it's maleficent forked dripping venom set with sights ready to ensnare.

Pull in the reigns industrially before the sun sets and it becomes too late,
place this bit upon that open sepulcher that you may never void control.
Take heed and hold steadfast that at the end you might have altered fate,
cast aside all malcontent to avoid the unseemly decimation of your soul.

Hearken to my wisdom; it is up to you, the relationships that get fabricated,
but it is also your free will that can take them, and leave them obliterated.

Will of fire

Caught in between the crash of waves and the dire straits,
when there is turbulence during your life's flight.
Will you engage your free will and become entangled with fate,
or will you just become consumed by the challenges blight?

Stoke the fires, work the bellows, push back the edge of dark,
this is a season to raise a fist to go forward with some gumption.
Don't just let your aspirations dissipate before you even embark,
put it into full-throttle so that there is no thought of submission.

Never fear the bumps that will occur in the road as you journey,
do not worry a moment of the retarded times of seemingly no movement.
You can take the heat after all you are not in the fire, you are the furnace,
keep adding the times you tried as fuel for your own improvement.

So, are you going to make use of that slowly churning ire,
by making serendipity in your life and showing your will of fire?

American ex machina

Coolant evaporates into the thin air of the mountains as a child breaths,
oil is poured into half a million vehicles as the seedling starts to grow.
Cogs and gears begin to turn as time rolls on forward unceasingly,
childhood assembles into adulthood leaving only the essentials to show.

If the adult is fragmented he still puts his pants on one leg at a time,
as he slips on his boots he begins the process of reconstruction inside.
If he were brought low with guns blazing he wouldn't retaliate with a crime,
he has maintained his morality through the decades and let it shine.

He still believes in excellence as you can tell with his every stride,
even though the bones may be broken, his stubbornness pulls him through.
People with their multiplying psychotic doctrines try to slay his pride,
not the pride of one's self but the pride in everything believed to be true.

Some might say he doesn't have a heart otherwise he would shatter,
others try to pick and prod to deduce to them what seems to be his insanity.
But the truth is he loves unrelentingly, race creed or color doesn't matter,
call him what he is, the god revering ever persevering American ex machina.

Abaddon

Gnarled Iron teeth-gnashing through the blood of the innocent,
the beast only known as Abaddon rises to tread all underfoot.
Awoken at last it crushes all underneath its bronze claws descent,
withered oaks line it's back, inferno breath turns the world to soot.

If you should see it's pale green glowing eyes, find a different direction,
the one who has the strength to slay the beast has not yet arrived.
Your hands' inability to penetrate it's tarnished scales for evisceration,
abandon hope all ye who see the beastly dragon and hope to survive.

A sheer monstrosity, and utter capacity to destroy with a single bellow,
death, and rot is its natural cologne that brings about its motivation.
Maleficent grotesque form leaves only the land of hades to follow,
a sinister cackle is the sole warning before it starts its vocation.

Abaddon is his name who gets drunk on the blood of the martyred,
the very utterance of his name leaves the world to quake in terror.

Sea of madness

The patrons come calling to ask how it is that my soul rests,
my vessel is cool, and collected to the unperceptive touch.
One by one the questions arise into focus like an unyielding test,
I graciously answer the one word fine as if it were close enough.

However if you had eye's unveiled maybe you could look deep enough,
to be able to see that not everything is as it is perceived to be.
That perhaps you would know my facade is just blocking my suffering,
really I am yearning to know the feeling of what it feels to be free.

That as it is, I'm flailing violently in turbulent rouge tides,
they boil, and churn of their own free will with intricate design.
My lungs are pressed to find the next breath, after all, I've cried,
with my mind racing at the question it's the right answer I try to find.

For you see my tormented soul is trapped within a sea of madness,
that no matter what I do I am incapable of completely stopping the ire.
Yet coincidentally slowing it down is where in which I have found my finesse,
being tossed to, and fro in this boiling sea of madness I have slowed the fire.

Black train

Octopi suction cups wrapped around the beating essence,
pulling its snare with the wrench grip down to the voided abyss.
The water sank in like a sieve under a waterfall of acquiescence,
sucking in ink filled with venom and pumping hastily into a hiss.

Sunken puffy eyes caught in the mist, it's the ears that hear,
the placid steam brakes of a train dressed down in fresh obsidian.
A conductor screaming out for passengers to come aboard the rear,
palpitations mixed with inebriation in a cocktail to make the fall in.

Quivering footsteps arching toward the rugged iron steps,
tremoring and holding a ticket to be punched for a final ride.
Clenching a veneer-thin piece of parchment out of their depth,
a slip of paper for a gaunt man reaching as he's tossed to his side.

A lone whistle blows like a whippoorwill caught in a spring song,
fading into echoes of voices as coughing bursts into fits of spasm.
Floods drain into ponds away from the hearts' fluid throng,
dodging a final ride of a skeletal train charging toward a chasm.

On fire

Flames spluttering and crackling as embers into a billowing breath,
exhausting its tinder as charcoal fissures into dust swept away.
Lips curved like a bow being stretched back at the archers' behest,
as ashen clouds begin their downpour to the chortle of decay.

Washed down into clay illuminated by the flaxen glow of steam,
coals blazing in an inferno rooted like a tree's tendril roots.
The scales of society exert their tax from the light of the dream,
spitting spires of flame off into the brackish night like bamboo shoots.

Ironwood cascades into fluttering fireflies made of sparks,
trying to transplant a seedling of fire into the chest of another.
Hot breath blowing a gust into fraying-soaked leaves spread apart,
sopped bark catching drops of water falling onto sisters and brothers.

Wind-streaked ruptures stained by fire and cloudbursts of the land,
though pyres burn brighter on bitter nights better in the roar of a choir.
The tar-slated road of a journey can be hard upon the feet to stand,
every flickering tongue of a sun drop singeing is worth being on fire.

Living in the rain

Washed down in salt drops under a canopy of graying treetops,
a pastel blur of colors swirling into the rainbow's hypnotic sway.
Coursing water dragging the spirals like a riptide into the rocks,
skin tremoring under a new magnitude earthquake of pain.

A paralyzing serrated blade plunged into the scabbard of the throat,
dressing the tongue in crimson for a meal seasoned in bitterness.
Regal to the eye with words in a double-breasted ducktail coat,
diplomatic charisma parting the rising tides with a staff of wit.

Camouflaging smiles to hide the silt slipping through fingers,
nostalgic pieces of dirt whisked away by gales of a sideways pour.
Flecks of refined gold trust whittled away as the flood clings,
silver-lined clouds that no ladder may reach from the earthen floor.

Drinking toxic swill from the still spout of dismay unaged by oak,
inebriated with the scent of amber frames of a distant memory stain.
Bane dipped thoughts dripping through the cracks onto the cloak,
pruned hands and feet as the testament of my life living in the rain.

Anger

To what is it that we equate our most substantial indignation?
Do your vain imaginings bring about scenes of coursing water?
Irrefutably beyond a shadow of a doubt on vexation, it is conflagration.
A storm of flame that consumes all stuck in its wake as it burns hotter.

When ignited all seems to be at a calm however, hungry are the cinders,
grasping onto whatever they may lay claim to use to slake their hunger.
Rapidly they grow to a disproportionate size to become a hindrance,
leeching off of every sound or foul thing to bring great things asunder.

Even when they run their sustenance dry, shriveling up into ash,
there exists a remnant of which will never truly extinguish.
Waiting patiently as an eagle eye trained upon a bass,
for that singular moment in which it can reflash.

Quite a quandary it can be with this fire,
but such is the psychology of ire.

The curse of silence

A void taking place inside the masses ear's is not
a blessing but rather a curse,
a curse they chose to inflict upon one another
as their sacred love grows frigid.
Whether it be a product of disproportionate
pride or totaling afflictions adverse,
blissfully unaware that we are unable to traverse
without the voice as a bridge.

Despite the wars stacked upon wars and the rumors
surrounding like a tidal wave,
the poverty of souls that we should feed with
knowledge and sustenance.
The hearts of the old and frail, that we should
be protecting to the grave,
all of this remains suspended in a chaotic storm
only known as the curse of silence.

How can we travail forward in this faux
tranquility of the human condition?
When everything persists in a continuous state of entropy.
When it simply has become too hard to open
one's mouth in their volition,
to where has it faded this humanity?

That we remain cascading in acrimony,
not having an ounce of tenderness.
To be stuck striving alone,
that is the nature of the curse of silence.

Dreams

A plethora of neural concoctions swimming in between electric pulses,
blood pressure surges upward as the mind begins its dream cycle.
Pinned in paralysis as the body struggles to gain hold, arteries convulse,
what is happening? Are the thoughts rushing through the internal psyche?

Caught in an abysmal display of abject horror or dreary melancholy,
one might query why things are to be this way when fast asleep.
I have often wondered if my dreams are hell or some purgatory,
where devils come calling to bargain in attempts to sift me like wheat.

Hideous cliché monsters come lurching forward out from the abyss,
life force dripping from the hands that remain eternally stained.
Ever pressing darkness of which the shadows come to make me recidivist,
being wrapped in chains to be dragged down until I become cremated.

Not once in a while do these things occur of which I hold disdain,
consistently hitting and missing days with a track record insane.
One might query if it is a lack of chemicals or something innate,
however, my theory is it's the consequences of one in deep-seated pain.

The deal

What could prompt such a rapid succession of events such as these, where one moment all is an orchestra of chaos, then the next a tall man in a suit.
Silence ebbs and flows in waves, nothing escapes not even the cool morning breeze,
dressed as the blackest night with a saw tooth smile ear to ear is the reason for the mute.

Eyes deadlock whether of resilience or a sense of being filled with vile dread, He breaks the standstill first with his eerie ominous voice uttering, "Don't be so uptight." Calm as a madman's lullaby he pulls out a set of the chairs from the air colored in Venetian red. He gestures politely yet menacing as if to instill a sense of obedience and fright.

He moderates his tone like a salesman's pitch saying, "I've come here because I like you." Keenly aware that isn't the case by his overall demeanor and stature.
Before you can properly assess the gravity of the situation he states,
"I've made a deal or two, so please have a seat my friend.
I'm not here for your end. I want to discuss a suture."

Unsure if you can decline, you traipse forward breaking line of sight for a moment only, regaining your vision on the mysterious stranger of other-worldly means you shudder. You're not sure if your eyes were playing tricks on you, but his visage turned hollow and ghastly. For a split second, you could have sworn he was horrifically burnt and heard a trace of thunder.

Resuming his speech, "good . . . I'm glad we could sit down and talk about this civilized. Now then son of Adam what is it you desire, fortune, fame, women, all are within my reach. I am the power of the air. I can manifest any poison mankind has ever contrived, filling the worldly needs of those in want is what you might say is my marketing niche."

Twiddling thumbs, you hope and pray silently this is all a night terror of soon you'll awaken, but he raises a brow and snaps his fingers assuring you with his overbearing voice, "I am real." A meager quiet voice pops out of you, "I don't need anything . . . but uh . . . thanks, any . . . way?"

Glaring, his pupils tighten making a snake's slit, stating, "I didn't come here for your beau ideals."

Eyes making you feel as though you were an ant trapped underneath a magnifying glass. If you could combust, you would certainly be incinerated by his gaze. Stammering, you get your next question out. "What exactly do I have to give in return, if I may ask?"

Smirking, as the corners of his mouth touch his ears.
"Your soul will I come back to raze."

Looking away you can't believe you're doing this, but it's not as if you could actually refuse, as you carefully say, "I want it all . . . everything, money, fame, women." Feeling ashamed. Giddy, he laughs in a multitude of voices as he takes out a contract completely obtuse. Taking a pin out of his right breast pocket, he says, "Blood always gives a true name for us to claim."

You prick your finger and touch it to the paper as the ringing goes off in your ears.
Opening a drowsy eye you slam your hand down on the off button of the clock to start the day. Getting up you walk to the bathroom glad it was only a dream, such a relief to your fears. As you hear your phone jingle, you walk back to see what it is while you were sleeping the night away.

A voicemail, but no missed calls. The thought of who it could be crosses your mind.
Dialing, you decide it would be best to hear what the message is after your night's wild ride. Entering your password, you listen in, as the voice reverberates to your deepest despair inside. "Just remember, I have delivered my end. So, at the end of 10 years there's no use trying to hide."

Cupid's arrow missed

Seated in pews of a catholic cathedrals congregation,
visions of the week prior invade with the exsanguination.
Black leather interior of a mid-sized sedan, only one life remained,
inebriation cut in twain the bond of two to leave one in pain.

Though he begged, he bargained, even offered up his soul,
there were no takers to spring forth and console.
He kicked and he screamed in all manner perverse,
not a soul found refuge from the storm of his cursing.

But of course this is just a bleak remembrance of the grim fact,
the one laid out not more than eight pews away was not coming back.
A crowd gathers with weeping and mourning for the dead,
yet silence consumes him even as hours later he lumbers into bed.

He seethes in vitriolic rage thrashing about, vehemently hissing,
roaring in temporal insanity that cupid's arrow must have missed.

Decadence

Upon the turning of the road an epiphany occurs, I am but mere dust,
for the present moment I appear in the shape of a man.
However as time passes me by, my bones and skin begin to rust.
Which shows the undeniable truth, I am just a gelatinous pile of sand.

Whence I have come, so too, I will return to the hands that made,
the hands that sculpted the earth from the dark lifeless void.
I glimmer with hope while the world worries of its empire to fade,
they question my joy and recommend I seek the help of Freud.

We are mere particles of dust floating on the wind,
their eyes are veiled and solely focused on matters only temporal.
Eyeing me like a canker, as some sort of morally inclined sin,
ears are closed with minds engaged in entertainment and euphoria.

They have blissfully hardened their hearts to be cast as anchors,
into the ocean of eternity to be dispersed by the underwater tidal rift.
Sand will deposit back upon the shore to never again be anymore,
while I still chose to believe those hands to save me from being sifted.

The phoenix and the dragon

The years continued to drain from the weakened sinew and flesh,
upon a dank evening; that boy ached to bring about blessing.
He was not of the oracles of the long-lost millennial years,
not a deity to call down celestial light to expel bane and fear.

Strands that bound her now were roots trying to absorb a cure,
dangling in the streams of fate, which not a person was sure.
The plight had come down swiftly as a non-chosen curse,
roots wove into a faded gown, the odds equal to life or a hearse.

Full head of vibrant dark hair had now become speckled with gray,
the boy gave everything, vision taught this may come one day.
In the spirit, the boy became a phoenix to fight a dragon,
the one enslaved by it was too frail to struggle in between its gums.

The Phoenix clawed and scratched weakening the dragon's grasp,
The bird of pyre defied hell followed by soot and ash.
Two creatures persisted to clash, the dragon seemed unfazed,
eventually, its jaw began to slack after months, weeks, and days.

I know it sounds like a tale from a prosperous time of yore,
the kind of story you expect a happy ever after like many before.
Regrettably one must confess this is only a poetic expression,
from a child in the glimpse of eternity who chose at discretion.

To describe a man's battle through sources of academia,
against his mother's ongoing fight with leukemia.

The only angel in hell

I was strapped upon a bolt of lightning,
first, contact with the earth and sprang up swinging.
Particle collider speeds stripped off the armor,
chained to the physical world no longer free of harm.

Cuts and punctures grew into scars to tell the tale,
of a being that knew not the definition of the word fail.
An outsider might suppose he was just a sinner,
that amidst his travels the straight road grew thinner.

Rusted that sword he clutched in his right hand,
a sword forged in the flames of anger time fanned.
Crow's feet marred the flesh around his eyes,
the tongue had learned a language that the world despised.

Some call him their favorite, some call him the worst,
for the language learned, was the truth that most couldn't endure.
The turning of the sphere couldn't earn him the title saint,
nor the relentless chain events that made him seem tainted.

He had metamorphosed into an angel of iron and flame,
that even whilst the entirety of the globe was going insane.
One that could not be blown about by the powers of the air,
as the story told, those grievous wounds were gotten by caring.

Carved into the tapestry of his body and weapon of option,
the battles fought in this sanguinary war of being incautious.
Only occurred to fend the weak against their usurpers,
despite the long line of accusers and countless precursors.

That rusted sword hoists him upheaving with breath almost gone,
an eloquence resounding of an almost symphonic song.
To the audience in the world's most true state of brimstone,
deep among the denizens of hell stood an angel all alone.

Eyes of ocean spray

Eyes of ocean spray leaping forward to cause delay,
shining smiles reaching out to draw you away.
Hands pivoting forth to and fro in a melancholy display,
entertaining the notion of lifting one up that's in dismay.

Reaching downward to one whose smile was as bright as starlight,
all was calm, however not for long as the day quickly turned to night.
Eyes of ocean spray transforming into a gloomy mire,
the smile of sheer radiance, now a distorted look of ire.

A hurricane of force couldn't seem to loosen the grip,
nuclear war seemed brighter than this relationship.
Holocausts of human history seemed less demoralizing,
the idea of moving away is almost patronizing.

Should you see eyes of ocean spray, discern a moment or two,
chances maybe, that those eyes want to drown you.

Her

These dreams collecting from respective streams,
peering back at me so elegantly. Have I seen what I need?
Is it true my heart is not my own to stow away?
That it has always been in another's hand to play.

That it was only just revealed today?
I seem to be at a loss that exists in a haze.
Could someone come and point the way?
Is that you that's come to do just so in your way?

My heart races as I pace and can't believe this is it.
How did I ever earn someone such as this?
Distinguished, refined, such loving kindness,
couldn't have hoped for more finesse.

Surely nothing has given me the merit to have her,
but since when is this world about things you deserve?

Artemis and her bow

Her gaze is as soft as fine silk and yet piercing like wrought iron blades,
the heart elegantly galloping in her chest not so to wisp out or fade.
Strength ripples from her clustered mind into sinew and flesh,
everyone with any sense knows she can't be bested.

Visage of femininity intertwined by a strength that makes me weak,
a goddess amongst the mere mortals that I wish to keep.

There exists not an iota upon earth that even compares,
the grace of her being or the strands of flowing hair.
Her aim is perfection and of this, all men very well know,
yet moreover, my eyes long only for Artemis and her bow.

The feeling

From the time I was young I searched for a lover,
whose grace and kindness radiated forth like no other.
Which the words had rang out from the crowd you will know,
how was I to know that her touch would feel like home?

That what I rigorously searched for was not so far away,
like the dawning of a new day, the gentle turning of a page.
There she was dripping with perfection so honey sweet,
that I swear to you she had the power to command the cerulean skies to weep.

What I yearned for deep in my being was right in front of me,
I froze in the midst of her earthy gaze, standing in fiery anxiety.
Thoughts crashing inside my head like rogue waves,
inferiority had come to show its face, causing my delay.

A kiss from those vivacious lips made that all turn ashen gray,
as she embraced me like a tidal wave, washing it all away.

The poets ink

The inquiry was poised serenely as a summit's precipice,
as simple and tranquil as a child amidst its innocence.
Inquisition that must have had answers etched in stone,
perpetuity before this happenstance in times song.

The question posed was, why is it that the poet's ink is black?
At first, it seemed not loaded like a colt 45. Aimed at the back,
hammer cocked and loaded, ready to spray out one's essence.
The gears began to churn, and with my mouth, I began to profess.

The reasoning of the poet's ink being black upon white parchment,
is that it is the elixir of the farthest most intangible parts.
Though not every subject be so daunting, dark, and dreary,
the black and white deliver a contrast to answer any inquiry.

As if the spirit itself were laid out as an unyielding scroll,
the ink is black because it is the darkness leaking from the soul.

The Man of Tripoli

There once was a man from Tripoli,
born into unyielding slavery was he.

Tormented daily by the increasing weight of labor,
save not a lover to which he could favor.

Pain, anguish turned into being hell-bent,
insanity twisting in from his inhumane treatment.

Until on one balmy mist filled summers eve,
eyeing the full moon far through the trees.

He wasn't sure what to pray,
whom he could call to save the day.

So he slit his wrists,
that someone might get the gist.
Vision slowly drifted into dark mist.

When an angel draped in light came in hushed,
at this show of succor, the man was touched.
Suddenly filled with static electric vigor and a rush.

He couldn't fathom that someone had come,
was this purely a mirage the abyss had done?

The angel said in a emerald shaded sickly sweet,
arise oh you of Tripoli to your feet.

I can break your hammer tempered bonds to set you free,
all you have to do is offer yourself on the altar of life to me.

The man eager to escape, nodded his head faster,
outpacing the archaic mages of legend with the spells they cast.

He steadily complied to every whim, meeting every demand,
to a verbal contract that only had the witness of the sand.

Before the angel departed he said what's fair is fair,
when your hair has silvered to winters glow, you'll leave your lair,
coming to find me where I hide, entreating you with care.

On the morrow the man's slaver had set him free,
promise kept, he was seemingly unshackled to live a life of glee.

Scarred and beaten he was oft seen as a heathen,
women refused him and children seemed to fear him.

Stuck in heavy manual labor,
he still seemed to find no favor.

The years passed treacherously on by,
finally unearthing where that dimly lit angel did hide.
His voice rose like unhindered flames accusing him of a ruse once inside.

Even though he wasn't a slave after a fealty act,
life was even more tar laden since the fact,
that the angel had come to help this simple jack.

The angel with his eyes almost In tears,
profane laughter echoed in waves through the clearing,
his mouth far-reaching beyond the ears.

Showing the razor Snell hook-like teeth,
It was then he began to speak.

I gave you years and alleviated all your fears,
eager you gave yourself to me, all in the hopes to be free.

Alas, you never queried my name.
But of course, now, it's all the same,
you were simply a pawn in a much grander game.

I tried to explain, yet you insist that I deceived you, much to your lament.
Yet I suppose if you're in such discontent,
feeling your time was worthlessly spent.

I could spare you this eternal anguish and pain,
as of course it is only but a game,
lure them in, we'll rack them up like billiards and play again.

American darkness

Darkness flows like a waterfall here,
though the sun basks this place the same.
So rampant, it will send you a shiver dear,
this land, oh this land surely has a name.

It seeps from their eyes, mouths, and fingertips,
as they divide to stand against one another.
However, it doesn't deter the merchants on their ships,
they lost how to love each other as sisters and brothers.

Clamoring they say it's the dream of this land,
to that, they cling even as they lower into a bottomless pit.
With the violence that leaves blood mixing in clay and sand,
someone needs to come to cast away the shadow critically.

Greed, malice, and all things wicked do they hark,
this is no ordinary abyss, it is distinctly American darkness.

Devil radio

Airwaves filled with familiar voices,
sinister overtones say don't touch that dial.
We've got an opportunity for your choice,
a boon like a crocodile hidden in the Nile.

Carnivorous teeth, jaws unseen, ready to devour,
charisma dripping like honey from every syllable.
Springing forth words of wealth and power,
a master of the universe is present, undeniable.

Decline, decline, decline the offer being made,
villainous intent is swirling near the glade.
Tempered phrases get forged into words of Hades,
the tongue in the static becomes a blade.

Time in this assault on the ears seems lost of reason,
flowing callously like the river Styx into the brain.
Sunlight fades through the dew and fabric creases,
the malevolence of a spirit unknown fades.

The conscious stirs to an idea perhaps crazy,
perhaps maybe that was the devil on the radio.

Funny

Funny how the world values money,
first appearances and all things sunny.

That the very word married,
is only a letter away from marred.

That if you disagree with one opinion,
a dark overlord has sent you, his minion.

That they all beckon for the truth,
yet in their turn, you must just be ruthless.

Funny how things turn out to be,
when the shoe is laced below another knee.

That they all wish to scream for equality,
but with a frown, insist upon chivalry.

The world is a funny place in this day to be,
picking definitions, based on individual situations you see.

Wisdom

You have to claw until you bleed through concrete,
just to have a warm aspiration of my heartbeat.

Past fibers crocheted together with whiskey,
scars telling a story, deeper when you see.

A hustle so flawless it's like I wrote the rules on monopoly,
those days, though, aren't forgotten even when I dream.

Some had to be baptized in the waters of Jordan,
I, however, had to be baptized when the flames began.

What works for people is often the roll of a die,
for me, it was the path of fire to open my mind's eye.

Drowning in a lake of alcohol, flailing to my mistakes,
eventually onshore, adding to my wisdom out of that lake.

Sin eater

A miasma of blackest pitch dripping like desiccated sewage,
from eyes, mouth, ears, and every other appendage.
It's darkness abhorrent like a torrential rain of tar,
behold, ladies and gents, the rancid sin eater from afar.

Eating the weight of the world off of everyone's shoulders,
making celestial light transport them to a world of no pain and warmth.
Yet who is it that comes for this lowly sin eaters Lamentations?
To lift them away from their wounds and lacerations?

Is it not so, one day a benevolent soul will have to descend into darkness?
Is it not also true that no creature can truly deserve such a thing as this?

That's just with all legends once bade.
That one day all flames,
must flicker and fade.
That turning of night,
into sweet light.
Must descend,
to its timely,
End.

Whiskey

Whiskey sipping gets me tipsy,
gives the finest of buzzes,
to dull the sharp world to fuzz.

W We always think of it as a way to party,
H but hardly do we think of the gravity,
I that results in depravity.
S We just look at the strong kick,
K from the shot we just took,
E getting hooked until we get nicked,
Y then we pick a hair of the dog,

put it back without so much a care.
whiskey sipping gets me tipsy,
gives the finest of buzzes,
to dull the sharp world to fuzz.
W But I know where the liquor can take you,
H quicker than you can bat an eye,
I your eighteen and the doctors say you might die.
S in that chair hearing your liver is in decline,
K But you don't care because the party isn't there,
E you're supposed to be the life of everywhere,
Y but here you sit, morally deficit.
stomach pumped and casually knocking on death row.

Whiskey sipping gets me tipsy,
gives the finest of buzzes,
to dull the sharp world to fuzz.

The collector

Bamboo splints under a fingernail,
such measures of force never fail.
Shattering knee's into splinters,
bring resistance to cinders.

Try to run and try to hide,
the collector comes tonight.
Try to bargain and lie your way out,
he's creative and ready to go any route.

Told every day that dead men can't pay,
he'll get the money, no matter what you say.
He's got a pickaxe ready to stake a claim,
the collector is coming to bleed the gold from your vein.

Man in black

White walls coated and padded in leather,
an institution of healing for the sick to get better.
Psychology though not really their bailiwick,
inept to find what makes mental disease tick.

A different time is what every expert says,
to justify the madness of the physician's heads.
Scooping out brains like an ice cream parlor,
leaving them drooling and dribbling, mouth ajar.

Next in line, an archaic device strapped to the head,
an example of credulous thinking of a backwoods shed.
A woman of Hebrew descent locked down for a ride,
electrified repetitively day in and by sleepless nights.

What could have possibly been this woman's crime?
That she was here like a death row inmate doing time.
For on this day she would be charged the ultimate price,
slain like a common cur she gave up her life.

All because she said way back when,
that she saw a man in black in her den.

Cocaine

Columbian snow or so everyone calls it,
it's a cavalcade of excitement in every hit.
A fortified rush from snorting dust,
only making you rust.

You think you're in control
yet you've traded your role.
A master of life's everything
now a puppet on a string.

You're washed and hung out to dry,
strung out like a war criminal to die.
Thought you could handle the addiction,
now you're seeking out benediction.

Black heart

When I was but a sapling in a world of oaks,
my heart was as pure as the freshly driven snow.
Time had not yet ravaged the core of my being,
but the hourglass stands still for neither pauper nor king

Time rained down with it, many changes of air,
new faces looking down with masks of care.
One mask came shattering to the floor,
a feeling of dread never felt before.

The time raining down came in tar drops now,
soaking in through skin with the confusion that abounds.
In the bloodstream, collecting right in the ticker,
filling up a glass of inky liquor.

Pumping through my veins was the need to write,
to let go of all the things so dark and contrite.
Who could have known it'd be this way from the start,
ink traveling to the page from my black heart.

Azazel

Tossed into a pit of gravel, then covered up with earth,
taught mortals the enciphered scripts of heaven for mirth.
You filthy specks of water and trace elements needed a Prometheus,
the enchantments with sparks of creation I showed you were ingenious.

Yet, here I lay face down on jagged rock sinking deeper in the dirt,
held captive in a prison of rage, with a fire freshly birthed.
I gave you the secrets of all the heavens themselves,
in turn, you morphed grotesquely into the true devils.

To me, they ascribe every carnal worldly sin,
be honest it belongs partly to your kin.
As I gave you use of every material in good faith,
your kind turned to evil and chose to raze.

So here I lay, near from the start,
but I won't be alone forever in the dark.

Dark and beautiful

The pitchest of blacks is my sweet enchantress,
a symphony of beauty that always impresses.
I Marc Antony and itself as Cleopatra,
exposing and capturing all my synapses.

How the cosmos couldn't begin to contain my joy,
when by happenstance I come on to a caliginous story.
Riddled with pain, sometimes traces of trepidation,
such things feed me the food to reach satiation.

One might be inquisitive of my love for inky black,
with glee, I'd be ecstatic that they asked that.
Not all souls have felt the release of a radiant gleam,
every personage has felt the Tartarean.

In the murky depths where hope is bereft,
we are joined together in that stygian mess.

Phantom Jack

A maundering loon enters in on a friendly dare,
one hand just minutes away from the midnight hour.
The chuckling fool not even remotely aware,
the phantom resident is almost at full power.

Ethereal darkness pulls on the intruder's nerves,
wisps of cobweb on nearly dry rotted lumber.
Echoes and groans broadcasting fear to the dupes every curve,
lost in time, its sole resident is slumbering.

Decrepit wood and decayed iron creaking agape,
to a miasma swirling in the tenebrous and calm parlor.
Clock clangs twelve as the door shuts behind his face,
foolhardiness has now molted its shell to be horror.

A mad dash back to the door met with a cancerous fault,
panicking to pry open the mouth of the forgotten entry.
Feeling thunderous heart palpitations when suddenly he halts,
hearing the meandering footsteps of the one in hegemony.

He tries to flee only to hear the sound from a different direction,
the source of the miasma now finally visible in full view.
Black holes for eyes concave nose, skin a leathery complexion,
mile arms to a torso frail, no lips showing razor teeth a new hue.

Frozen he stands as phantom jack finally comes out of the haze,
Jack shoots in his boney fingers to impale the boys' midsection.
Gouging, ripping, and tearing out internal organs in a craze,
today the fool learned trespassing at jacks is a mortal sin.

Western skies

For ages, I saw the same decrepit crystalline sky,
the same mundane thing with clouds to deliver a sigh.
As I sit on the western front it is all but the same,
where it rolls on for miles remaining yet untamed.

Like a wild cat in a frenzy, it remains uncaged,
even in the midst of society relentlessly turning the page.
It is always never the same with gentle hints of blue,
casual as a gentleman caller, it smiles at you.

Cotton candy clouds that almost seem to touch the ground,
the sky here is different or so I have found out.
It hardly lets loose a drop of moisture from its chamber,
which at times for the land can be a danger.

Near the twilight hour, it becomes a canvas of pigments,
the kind of ornate display that leaves the eye's drenched.
Not from pain or misery but from pure celestial grandeur,
that leaves a lasting impression of one last thing pure.

Love questions

Life is about minuscule changes set to a scale,
my friend this is true, I tell you no gargantuan tales.
Life is a funny mistress filled with many quirks,
many of which will leave you in the dirt hurting.

So allow me if I may with my inquisitive mind,
to make some inquiries upon you to see what I find.
What happens when you'd rather break than bend?
World looking on with blind eyes and thoughts condescending.

Would the world believe that when the wind blows one way,
out of pure spite, you walk the other to the next day?
Tell the truth and let someone grieve rather than shield them?
Mend broken hearts instead of allowing hatred to stem?

What would family think if you loved someone you shouldn't?
Yet you chose so anyway because your heart said you could?
Deep down inside your soul, you knew it was meant to be,
alas, your family said that you should remain free.

What would you see if you took a gander at me?
When you see these cowboy boots resting under this tree,
staring upon a lush green valley past the range,
dreaming about times past and things that might seem strange.

How would you react if you knew you couldn't change me?
when you know who I was through all the open seasons.
That you realized to change me would also destroy me,
would you keep me close in arm or set me free?

The one

Her skin is as luxurious as cashmere,
a wild rose of a soul with no fear.
Knew she was the one at happenstance,
hair golden as the sun shined just so by chance.

A heart unsmeared with rebellious choices,
mind unfettered by a statement of voice.
A grace familiar to the most ornate of angels,
eyes that entreat and entrance like a spell.

Her voice as sweet as vine-ripened grapes,
a life that is unfamiliar with the choice of hate.
Too bad, she can't come to the phone right now,
the seals of Solomon suddenly don't seem so sound.

All she had to do was listen to her friend's vision,
however, that would have hindered my mission.
Wearing her like a glove is exactly what I've come to love,
both hands are on the steering wheel while she suffers.

Stretching this girl out like Leonardo DaVinci's canvas,
the portrait I'm to paint will make sure we're both damned.
She will remember that day and always rue,
because now she is my human leather three-piece suit.

Autumn in New Hampshire

Clear mountain streams surrounded with yellow,
red oaks, sugar maples filled with delicacy.
Evergreens unyielding as the region embraces fall,
preparing for winter, and its snow not halting.

Days are tepid falling off into an ice blue freeze,
colors of orange, red, and yellow yield those from cities.
All life forms embrace this beauty of autumn,
the crisp air, sights truly ornately haunting.

Apple cider flows into glasses most freely now,
festivals, carnivals, things of dreams abound.
Camping, hunting with their accompanying fires,
this is a glimpse of autumn in New Hampshire

Born in heaven

Entrance to the world perhaps unusual to the common eye,
a child born under temperature with three sevens in place.
Such a thing could only be the roll of a well-rounded die.
Yet here it occurs in a clay, and iron world filled with haste.

Days passed as cars on a freeway with not a second lost,
a child is seen on the side of an oak infested mount.
Calm as the wind before a front contemplates the cost,
uncertainty in the mind of this boy truly comes to abound.

Months passed by like lightning striking the earth,
a teenager was removed and relocated to a wooded vale.
Collected, he looks out still focused on cost and his birth.
He wishes to return to his version of Eden in this tale.

Years ebbed, and flowed right on by with nary a wink,
A man now positioned in a recliner of a far away den.
Thoughts clashed into one another as he continued to think,
all this time, though he was poor he had been born in heaven

The road to here

The infernal power burns within my chest,
tetragram in place holding it close to my existence.
Its darkness almost enough to bring cardiac arrest,
filling up the void like gushing water into a crevice.

Like a fire eating its way through my throat,
I choke back the words I so longingly wish to say.
Aura seemingly of light but really being black smoke,
pushing back with all my might, I keep the demon at bay.

The power to raze anything to soot and ash,
with a flick of my tongue resting behind tight lips.
The Plutonian notion to destroy anyone in a flash,
gnawing its way forward through twitchy fingertips.

I came a long way from my unique suffering as a child,
blasting off like a rocket sent from somewhere in the deep.
It truly has been a long winding road to the meek and mild.
the demon though is not dead, just firmly restrained in my keep.

A book by its cover

Upon the blood-stained sullen road of perdition,
many are contrite traversing souls in recidivism.
Some are too far gone to find their repentance,
a few narrowly making the requirements of penance.

Countless in number line up to be sorted before a pit,
wailing in trepidation and sorrow of a bottom they'll never hit.
This tear-washed road that unnumbered meander,
soundtrack of grinding teeth, blasphemy and slander.

Upon the gory sullen road of gravel named perdition,
there exists one with his hand down to fulfill a mission.
Look up and see the truth and all that it offers in vision,
existing with tattooed flesh he exists to save the soul from ignition.

Grab the hand of a man who was once in that darkness,
the realm where no light penetrates that they confess.
The lord from the land of light saw fit to save him from damnation,
so an added hand could come to save from true excommunication.

Chosen to be redeemed by the lord beyond the sky in love,
reaches for you in foresight seeing more than a book by its cover.

The creature in the pit

The black pit beckons from behind closed eyes,
Tartarean chains rise from it, dragging everything down.
A place that rests nowhere near adjacent the sky,
the murky darkness so thick you could drown.

Those chains were wrapped around every limb,
there's no escape so why not just enjoy the ride.
Chains growing ever tighter into the skin,
this kind of sleep makes you wonder if you died.

Yet so in this place is a candlelit flicker just ever so,
illuminating a face of reptilian likeness in its glow.
Its eyes glowing red, piercing as near molten daggers into snow,
nose concaved, scales desiccated making uneven rows.

You try to move, you try to scream into the ink,
the sound reverberates into a deep abyss of nothing.
The creature only reacting in ways to make you think,
it's keeping a watchful eye on its prey where it is king.

It's oxymoronic docile approach, with its stare voraciously biting into the soul,
lulls one into a false sense of security to be petrified in its snare.
That if one keeps an eye on it, it will leave you solus,
but with every blink, it creeps until it's next to ear and hair.

Quivering in pure unadulterated horror at this freak,
a voice of crushing gravel whispers you belong to me.

Of the night

Soul basking in the darkness,
the most meticulous muse.
A forthright witness,
with so many hues.

Lost and found in the murk,
an anchored homestead.
Suffused with hurt,
all in the head.

Heart wounded by its heel,
unable to tread at pace in the light.
Weaving words in hopes to heal,
rebirthed as a babe of the night.

Soul permeated by ethereal shade,
the staunch afflatus.
Briefest of moments does it fade,
only in eternal rest may it be slain.

Episode of psychosis

Hell breathes with anticipation,
flames licking perspiration.
Voices drip nectar to the ear,
the lobes eat it dispelling fear.

A heart thunders through flesh,
flushed with everything but rest.
Closing the eyes is but a test,
that if it is done improperly, the next breath may be death.

Sweat pours from every pore to the floor,
like a hurricane just reaching the shore.
Meanwhile winding up through the cracks,
chains methodically coming to take something back.

Wrapping around everything in nooses,
dragging it down ruthlessly.
Down the spire,
into a fire.

Demons of vanity

Razor wire teeth arranged in rows,
eyes as the pitches of coals.
Leather skin wrinkled by insanity,
even these creatures love vanity.

Invisible by the light of day,
they follow closely in its rays.
Hairs rising to a needle's point,
their wrath is really the flip of a coin.

Infatuated by those who stand in mirrors,
their voice a gurgling ooze none can hear.
Paper-thin hands reaching out for beauty,
claws digging into their loot.

Careful they will even introduce themselves,
narcissistic love of self is their glittering wealth.
Coming in nights of sackcloth to their prey,
through the mirror they will drag you away.

The Ether

Swirling masses of ancient darkness,
smoke billowing from the agape hole.
Invisible hands pulling on every witness,
yet there is no flame, nor any frigid cold.

Teeth grinding echoes along the walls,
an obsidian orb punching and almost shattering the silence.
A child's whisper is heard as they fall,
melodic, callous, yet still a siren.

Swirling masses circle around the void,
drawn to the arcanum etching itself in floundering minds.
Few resist as they succumb to being destroyed,
no screams are heard as they leave the world behind.

The hole that is swallowing humanity whole,
human ego erased by the pit and the unrelenting hunger.
Never waxing or waning in size, dread begins to grow,
none ever hit the bottom with a clap of thunder.

Only one remains in the world as its human feature,
so when will you leap into the ether?

The corner of every eye

Light pervades into the perceived globe,
trickling in through the cracks of the atmosphere.
Tree's photosynthesizing while life unfolds,
yet in the corner of every eye, something appears.

Something never truly seen beyond a glimpse,
a mirage of shadow gone in a blink like a smoke wisp.
Terrifying little creatures they are when reality hits,
snared in sight, the beholder is prone to paralyzing fits.

Magnet tar oozes among their sinewy frame,
drawing your gaze to it like a law of nature.
Its visage is known to drive one to be insane,
as the tar peels backward revealing the enclosure.

Drenched in a effervescent putrid smell of the grave,
now chained invisibly by desiccation.
A simple turning of the head will make them go away,
a cautious hunter who feeds by petrification.

Locked in as the tar fully disappears,
revealing empty eye sockets with no eyelids.
Jagged teeth grinning at the prospect of fear,
the mind goes entirely absent from the prospect of dying.

No choice but to watch with a barren flame,
until you twist back seeing what they become.
Ancient leather now lines their elongated frame,
emaciated its bones rattle and creek for their morsel to succumb.

Now for a short span, they will hunger no more,
no one will be perceived to have gone missing.
As after they have consumed their gore,
they'll be in photos with family and friends wearing their skin.

The reflecting pool

Standing in water knee deep,
I see a reflection of me.
Yet not as others see.

My pneuma looks hideous,
dare I say even insidious.
A past with mistakes most grievous.

Forgive me for not seeing light,
when all I've ever known was night.

Lovecraft

Our story begins on a night just like any other,
a tale to be told blanketed by the stars' cover.
An eyelid drooping lad stumbles on down the road,
feeling frost at the back of his neck in October's cold.

A frigid breath blew across ragged tree's in the dark,
a nasty trick that almost gave the boy an upstart.
Picking up the pace with thunderous steps echoing,
asphalt lines the moonless nights beckoning.

Without missing a step his feet just naturally fell into place,
paranoia ripping through his brain leaving his mind racing.
It was almost as if a puppeteer were pulling the strings,
the mind befuddled in the dark will create some insidious things.

It was then his feet felt the splashing of sand on the beach,
head exploding in words that sounded like God and the devil each.
Wasn't long before he was knee-deep in water chilling his soul,
what his mind was incapable of realizing, was he hadn't far to go.

Numbing him so he couldn't even feel his breaths as he treaded water,
hours passed until he finally succumbed to an icy blue and faltered.
Slumber grabbed hold of him as he heard a clap of thunder in the deep,
wrapped in darkness and further into hyperthermia did his body steep.

The last his brain could record before it rusted away into madness,
as his body systematically shutdown to the last stage of death.
That brumal clap of thunder seemed akin to a colossal heartbeat,
like that of an old one stirring way down in the crushing deep.

Now that you've been told this tale of madness,
feel the joy? The overwhelming gladness?
That's our merciful dark lord who has chosen you.
Come with us to enjoy the nectar of his truth.

Because as it's been said,
by many who were clear of head.
"That is not dead which can eternal lie,
and with strange aeons even death may die"

Hallows eve

Hallows eve calls out from beyond the setting suns hue,
leaves rustle across the loam by a caressing breeze.
Trees stripped of their foliage which lay beset by early dew,
light now stretching like a dream into a twilight sea.

Serenity hangs in the air floating down in ataraxia,
as darkness paints the sky into the blanketed ebony.
Every mind humming the symphony of a dream,
while the morrow is still coming down by spider ivory.

Whereby three a.m. the spirits have arisen to face day,
called forth by archaic magic long since binding.
That comes crashing down as a ionic gas tidal wave,
fueled by the mirth of fear that is blinding.

Daylight fades back to a devilishly vicious night,
where demonic possessions run consummately rampant.
The desiccated dead claw at the dirt to feast by starlight,
the hope of daybreak becoming unreservedly non-existent.

Timber now rattling, transforms into twisted kindling,
pulsating with black-hearted contempt for the living.
The aromatic autumn with its blackened whisper of wind,
threading the spaces in between, latching on to maleficent giggling.

You who hides until such terrors cease to arrive,
you are never alone with the ticking of your clock.
Even you have a guest among you this night,
don't be rude and let loose your horrified thoughts.

In illumination, they dissipate like mist on the air,
though only since you inhaled their essence there.

The Consumption

Decay writhes through and around every structure,
the concrete, rebar, it crumbles like wheat being sifted.
Colorless, odorless, and gaseous it eats like an acid tincture,
once this was a land of opportunity for talent and those gifted.

Now it simply evaporates away out of existence,
the market square is now just patches of dirt and rubble.
Sealed off by man for what they unearthed in the insistence,
no screams were heard, it razed the area into less than stubble.

Fires sprouted up like weeds in June across the land,
snuffed out into the heat and soot that aided the corrosion.
A phantom blaze that left nothing with the capability to stand.
Such now is the bleak drawing upon this place in conclusion

Death and dismay as they withered away into mummified remains,
modern technology only left them bereft of hope and in confusion.
This could have been fiction if that miner's hand left instead of stayed,
that day down in the mines when they found the consumption.

Halloween in New England

Here on the river streaked mountains of New England,
foliage in colors deemed to be an artist's dream.
Parents buy sugary treats that children utterly demand,
dressed in costumes to play tricks for a little scream.

Words of caution to float into the ears of the wise,
should you find your feet standing on the eastern coast.
Buy a costume or just don a mask for your eyes,
loom it together if you must to even just be a ghost.

Gather the courage in your mortified thunderous chest,
stay out of the frost of this treacherous night if you can.
Blubbering from torturous murders echo through the air at rest,
they want an overflowing harvest from the green man.

Deep in their bowels they all lust for coffers filled with coin,
maple sap doesn't flow without the blessing of a greenman's touch.
Weaving a finite amount of costumes to know who joins,
children without skin, stained by the earth, now hushed.

On this blood-soaked night, the hand of death looms,
come by coach or air, just don't forget your costume.

The eyes of Ra

Liquifying through reinforced nano-enhanced fibers,
eroding away mankind's carbon coated steel.
Crosshairs locking onto deep space divers,
wrapping around the unsuspecting with tendrils.

Scanning every variable, surpassing any machine,
an acrid nature that stings the spine with bitter piety.
Bubbling with a putrid animosity in the spaces between,
burning into scoffing prey that is soon seized by anxiety.

Mayday, mayday ground control we repeat,
we have been taken over by coup d'é-tat.
We should have watched where we tread our feet,
the crew is under the control of the eyes of Ra.

Silence billows from the other end of the computer,
perplexed, all at control scramble to hear another word.
The overwhelming expanse of emptiness was hard to refute,
static crackled, only receiving dread from what they heard.

Jaws slacked until they fell open to the sounds after the distress,
calm, charismatic, the Faustian voice came in its Sunday best.

Ground control this is space exploration team Horus,
tangos have been neutralized of their coup d'é-tat.
We have begun a launch home, the falcon is soaring,
mission successful we have obtained the eyes of Ra.

Apprehension swallowed the essence of their atman,
as it occurred that wasn't the vocal cords of their captain.

The devil in the details

Cursive litters a page of parchment,
words overflow like the edge of a swollen river.
Eyes get lost in the ripples of its current,
that flow as if freely fed by supernal delivery.

Alabaster dotted in ebony ink shows pure contrast,
in the cardinal black and pure white, life doesn't provide.
A contract that will resurrect anything from the past,
provide for the future or give you something to hide.

Sign here you see and life can be carefree,
from LSD to the strips of Vegas with money.
Loose men or women, whatever helps sin abound,
miss mommy or daddy, we can always pull them down.

Wanna be famous, why not, let's go be shameless.
If you wanna be rich or if you're dying to get hitched.
Maybe see how far you can stretch immortality,
be like aqua man and really control the sea.

Abandon all hope who sign here on the dotted line,
because once crossed, your essence you leave behind.
In the end, don't say I didn't warn about my advantage,
you seed of Adam, which is cattle to befall carnage.

The pulse quickens like a rabbit taken off in a field,
a universe of possibilities only for the beyond to ail you.
Crumple it up to throw it away and truly heal?
Or embrace the devil in the details as your truth?

Dreams a cacophony

Dreams a cacophony,
vivid concoctions in the full spectrum.
Saturated in failures and misery,
yearning for a distant hum.

The ocean of black is preferred,
leaving the vivid for the obscured.

To dive into that squid's ink,
is a divine blessing to the eyes.
The inverse a galaxy of terror in sync,
night terrors of demons in disguise.

Paralyzed in place by an ethereal chain,
a towering dark figure looms over the chest.
Who knew in some you can even feel pain,
seeing a demon forcibly try to imbue you with his crest

Mortifyingly horrible imaginings of the deep,
dreams a cacophony of haunting things in my sleep.

Sirens call

Beware their angel tones,
the distant echoes offshore.
Thoughts ricochet in the cranium dome,
of waters never imagined before.

The eyes mesmerized by pastures unseen,
coffers and banks fill up with money.
Pantries restock themselves with sugar and cream,
the land while you walk hand in hand is always sunny.

Though as the fence is topped to a field barren,
where spare change can seem like a king's ransom.
Neither a nook nor cranny for a crumb of food to be caught in,
the very earth tries to devour you in quicksand.

The tales were not wrong,
the sirens are amongst us all.
Everyday situations are their song,
beware of their oceanic call.

My suture

The essence of the goddess in my eye,
a quintessence bathed by shimmering lights.
Skin as tender as freshly ground cocoa powder,
lips as vivacious as sprinters for a finish line.

Touch is that of fine Ethiopian cotton,
with those eyes shimmering their waterlogged clay.
They are gravities maw, in and of themselves,
as the mind gets sucked into elated thoughts.

A vision in black marble never to be recreated,
Davinci himself would lay brushstrokes for her smile.
Plato would never question her form,
for she is just as timeless as fate.

The breathtaking woman of my future,
for every wound, you've been my suture.

Cosmic chess

The devil,
reaches for the saint.
To strike a deal for revelry,
on this rock swimming in a cosmic constraint.

A chessboard,
souls sauntering in by design.
Hands fashioned to the marionettes cord,
most are pawns, some are lucky to be a kingly line.

The saint,
questions the rules at play.
Dancing to the rhythm of a concrete pain,
answers still materializing that might appear one day.

The ninth circle

Flames flickering to the rhythm of the earth breathing,
confined to the window view of a fireplace hearth.
Ice claws at blurred glass streaked by frost creeping,
snow falls swirling into a frenzy over the earth.

The world whites out into a blank sheet of paper,
ponds freeze to the footsteps of Judas Iscariot.
Oak wood-framed window sill etched by saber,
abandon all hope ye who enter here by their affairs.

Alabaster creeps down to strangle out the flickering flame,
Satanic fingers digging into the pneuma, driving in the nail of misery.
A shack of a cabin encased in an arctic prison freezing in its bane,
as a guttural grinding voice echoes this be the price of treachery.

The last rider

Hooves shatter the crisp frost laden grass as if it were glass,
chains wrapped around paper-thin ivory ligaments gripped tight.
A rattling of iron against cured bone akin to a sea of tolling brass,
the sockets of the rider are gaping holes filled with permanent night.

His skull barren yet still carved into a deathly haunting simper,
flesh and sinew a distant memory as his cheekbones echo a cackle.
Sound slicing into the night like a blade into a harvest apple so tender,
followed in stride by rivers of fire nipping at mortals like starved jackals.

The skeletal steed snorts out near liquid hell essence,
as the bone and hooves trek endlessly through dimensions.
The rider extends his scythe reaping the earth of any luminescence,
souls cut down like wheat to be sifted for the harvest collection.

The human race is off in the distance short-sighted,
nearly burnt away by the blue flames rising through the fallen.
Flickering, sputtering into new hosts for eternity's blight,
with a lone last rider gaunt and soaked in darkness riding for us all.

Prometheus's revenge

Desert yellow eyes pierce through the graphite black of an open door,
a sandstone with serpent slits that call out without uttering words.
Rows of teeth smile radiating a glow from the ceiling to a barren floor,
sharp, contented, a dim light that outlines a passageway absurd.

Feet move beyond despite an iron will that objects to the path,
shoes scrape the worn wooden floor as they dejectedly march forward.
Knees shaking like rocks in an earthquake before a creature of wrath,
the child passes through a daunting wood and gypsum fjord.

The voice with a gravity of Jupiter echoes through the hall,
the Machiavellian mouth of its owner hung as still as a painting in a museum.
"Come here my quivering pet and witness my most favorite part of all,
my fountain of joy is to watch you wither and fade in my colosseum."

A button nose of the child breaching in through the door,
etchings in glass illuminated by the full moon's light descending.
"Once I gave fire that breathed life like no other god before,
through my smoke and flame the metal of mankind is bending."

"I've trekked the mountains of Olympus from above the clouds,
so my eyes could witness my gift in humanity flicker out."

Crossroads isle

Through the forgotten overgrown fields of alfalfa and weeds,
the hangman's willows infested with spanish moss laying affixed.
Rests a house on a barren patch of dirt that listens to your needs,
the cornerstone carved out of obsidian from the bed of the river Styx.

Door dry rotted into dust carried off by many winters turbulent flurries,
once inside the sand in the hourglass will seem to refuse to fall.
As bleached pine transforms back into mahogany as rich as curry,
particles of furniture time wiped away reassemble in the peripheral.

A sea of footsteps echo, yet one lone man stands behind a desk,
steel-blue eyes refuse to mirror the invitation of his hearty smile.
His voice as soft as freshly churned butter from a face statuesque,
"good eve stranger, welcome to this humble abode known as crossroads isle."

"We have in stock many a vendor to give any earthly aid,
allow your mind to wander into the needs where we can shed a light."
The door casually walked through now a solid wall blockade,
the master will whisk it into being when he comes up at midnight.

Silence thickens in the room like rising dough before the oven,
broken like a rock under a stonecutter's chisel in timed strikes.
Bellowing from below toward the one with the racing heart coveted,
pounding of hooves from the master of crossroads isle at midnight.

The lady of the tempest

Southeast coastline hammered into by rain as heavy as lead,
the trees sway to a haunting tune conducted by the gales.
Timber creaks and cracks to the tempest rearing its head,
the water piles up like dirt reaching for the window veil.

Lightning crashes down almost as if from the hand of Zeus,
instantly lightbulbs explode apart like firecrackers.
A home now drown in a pit of darkness for the obtuse,
when through the wails of the wind comes a ladies laughter.

Windows crack behind the wood barricading them in,
laughter starts pouring through the walls like a storm surge.
A home now brewing as the tea kettle of madness in her kitchen,
contorting as a circus performer into a maze humming a dirge.

Walls turning into tar strips latching onto feeling hands,
another flash of lightning reveals the green-eyed maiden.
Yellow tubular teeth like a zipper track against white sand,
grinning as wide as the gulf coast, marching forward like fate.

Claws stained crimson stretched out like a rose from a lover,
the hurricanes were never the reason people left every year.
They flee a spindly lady who comes under the typhoon's cover,
for the lady of the tempest feeds on madness and fear.

Infatuation

Eyes dripping crude tar from the obsidian orbs into black streams,
highlighted against velvet eggshell skin lacking even a bead of sweat.
A body curvy like the mountain roads of a New England dream,
painted onto the earth by the stone still hands of an ancient set.

Fingertips laced with venom tracing the skin into temporary hearts,
lips with belladonna and wolfsbane smeared in a gloss, pulse racing.
Vision miraged by diamonds and gold as the turning sands art,
legs quivering for the touch of its tempter to set lust into ablaze.

In morning light after the night filled with devilish delights,
the fire of that night now dwindling into snickering embers.
Embers that burn holes into the fabric of a celestial rite,
leaving the heart as barren as the burnt fields of December.

Eyes in the dark

The eyes stabbing through the dark like knives,
irises whited out by a blizzard of the unknown.
Anxiety gripping a child like a vise squeezing tighter,
whispers traipsing up bed posts to one meant to be alone.

The voices slithering through invisible forked tongues.
"Hey, wake up, we want to see you, give us your light."
A spinning record set in a loop for an eerie song being sung,
hands clawing at covers trying to rip them off in the night.

Serpents gathered round with decaying lifeless eyes,
inching closer, creaking the wooden floors of an old house.
Syllables growing harsher and more coarse, quivering the thighs,
at the tender age of four, the events could send a chill up Faust.

Many moons have passed since that moonless December night,
yet even still the ocean of pure white eyes still gives me a fright.

Ode to misery

Misery, oh misery how your calloused hands embraced me,
gripping tightly to a child born dead and then revived to sickly.
Your icy touch through your bone fingertips dug deep into my side,
though years came unannounced they left me with a leathery hide.

Through the changing seasons, I thought you were my betrothed,
as your absolute zero, Jupiter gravity grip left my heart enrobed.
Your tendrils wrapped around every inch of my being since it began,
ripping away joy from me like paint at the blowing of sand.

What I had never understood was that you were a choice,
a despicable ailment in my bones to be dispelled by my voice.
We had our time in that tar pit prison where you like to keep me,
but now our hourglass has run out of sand and I am finally free.

The house of deaths' requiem

Fingertips flow down a corridor as brushstrokes from a horsehair brush,
painted as such in an eggshell white mixed with hues of magenta.
No bulb filaments were lit up orange, darkness almost telling the light to hush,
red mahogany wood laid out like a puzzle under each foot's center.

The eyes in a barren home following a trail to a black-framed doorway,
a brass handle can almost be heard whispering "come to see the gifts."
As a scarred up unsteady hand turns the knob to reveal an empty floor,
his unsure legs carry the man into a garage where reality rips.

Head panning to the left interior walls, the same his fingers traced,
when a benevolent voice springs in from the void, lingering on still air.
Eyes creaking over toward the voice as his heart begins to run a race,
showing a man stocky and large in a suit that sprang from nowhere.

The man had eyes that seemed as though they'd been ripped from a dragon,
a smile camouflaged as a lamb, with the razor teeth of a wolf.
Offering outwardly resurrections in the sincerity befitting a nun,
yet upon decline, the costume of the saint fell off to reveal his hooves.

The two wrestled in bloody combat like in the days of the coliseum,
the man though he gave all his strength, death still sang his requiem.

Doors

A room colored in granite and barren save only a door,
echoes of western boots against the oak drained of color.
The turning of the knob reveals a new space in rainbows glory,
black and white vanish in embers showcasing a sullen fjord.

Standing on the cliffside as the peripheral sees the door vanish,
lavish green knee-high grass tickles the knees through faded denim.
Eyeing the field of the cliffside leads feet to an entrance lavish,
draped in gold, symbols in royal sapphire from an ancient plenum.

Stepping through the archway to a bedroom filled with blacklights,
Zebra print lines the bed as nerves petrify into a living stone.
A voice comes through at first soft as a lady of the night,
whispering ineffable things as trekking feet sink to inaudible tones.

Falling through a painted movie set sideways into graphite,
eyes darting open, body drenched in sweat to midday light.

Harvey

Rain torrentially fell down as the water continued to rise,
chained in place by the wind swirling around in the southeast.
Teardrops added to the deluge as they streamed from eyes,
a hurricane held by celestial hands, a flood fed by a water droplet feast.

Cars and houses swept up like dirt into an enraged gods dustpan,
wind howling with water growing faster than weeds in midsummer.
It was the shattering of marriage like a rock through a glass lamp,
with the spiked shards penetrating ever deeper into the old thumper.

Tendons ripping apart in a right knee as easy as water-soaked paper,
stiffening harder than pig iron forged in the very flames of the sun.
Placed in a wrought iron brace forcing it to walk through coursing water,
nature let loose her fury upon me like a marksman with a gun.

Yet even though pictures and clothes washed away into dust,
a castle of sand sifting down into nothing at high tide.
Wood floors buckled up into ripples of pine dotted with rust,
left with a muscle warping into the shape of a tear as I cried.

Racing thoughts

Life has been a raging war fought inside of my head,
a coin toss with the duality caught between light and dark.
Bloodshed filled me to the brim in between the ears in its stead,
soldiers firing their rifles and starting a race of arms.

Artillery launching up thousands of shells keeping me up at night,
thoughts thundering like the atomic blast of hydrogen bombs.
Coursing shockwaves of electricity through my veins in shock and fright,
fire spreading through my chest like napalm in Vietnam.

Worry and doubt consuming me like paper pulp in sulphuric acid,
eating me alive like starving civilians caught in active war zones.
Whiskey was the burning elixir that kept my nerves placid,
quieting my trembling fingers like a mother's hum that drones.

Soaking in the still of star-filled skies, hands seek to scribe the battles fought,
as those shaking tendons attached to hands describe racing thoughts.

Internalized emotion

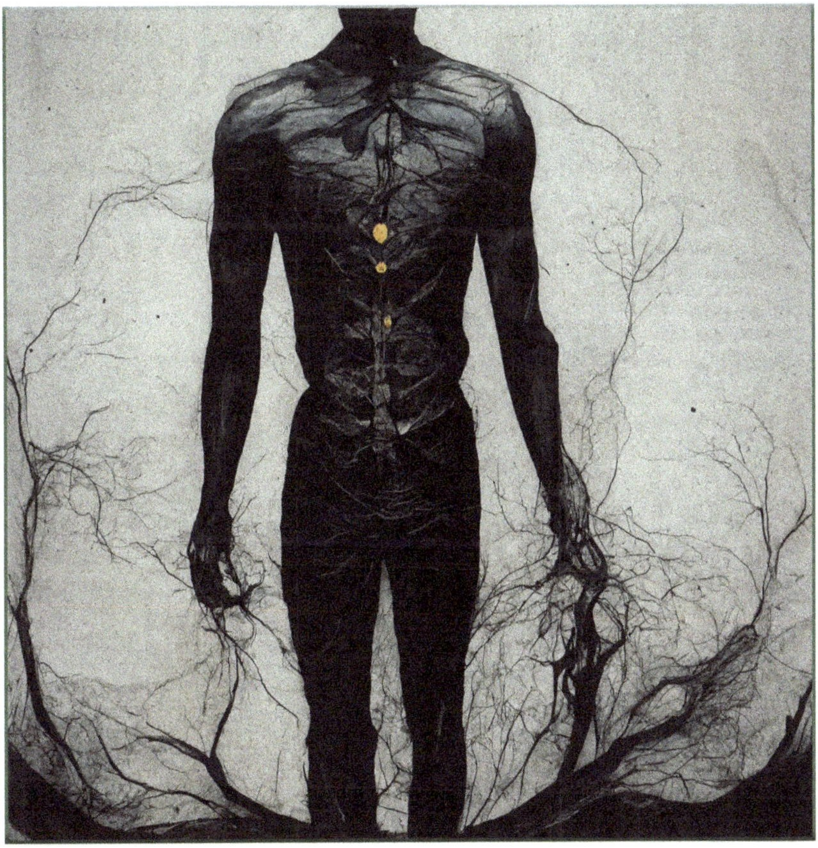

Swallowing gallons of bubbling black tar laced emotions,
ravaging the natural beatific gold and crystal hearts of the ocean.
Dripping down the back of the throat like an acidic nasal drip,
strapped down onto gurneys for rides into the hospital trips.

Years of wolfsbane swallowed down at societies request,
blood drizzling down to pool into the churning sea of digestion.
Injections of the poppy flower to take sight back from television static,
men, women in clean white coats and scrubs stare at the masochist.

A man stripped of clothing lost in a fog finally with an anchor,
lowering sails momentarily avoiding the rocks, keeping to the sandbank.
Taking port at the run-down dock, trudging to the lighthouse on the hill,
swinging open a battered gray wood door to a table, ink well, and quill.

A vision on how to purge the venomous sewage-filled sea,
opening the floodgates of the dam releasing out the black water tide.
No longer swallowing the elixir of lead-laced ink, withholding poetry,
putting pen to paper so that a hurricane of emotion in a glass bottle can die .

Desert sunset

On that day she left me to freeze,
in an arctic world.

What she forgot is that my people,
already knew how to survive,
after the desert sun went down.

Night writing

I ink pages at night,
for my tongue is blighted.

My hands open rusty iron cages,
dismantling archaic locks with haste.

So that my emotions may run free,
In a world where everyone can interpret me.

Doc Holiday

As age creeps to my face,
the more I transform into Doc Holiday

Devil's proposition

The devil propositioned me a carefree life,
instead, I chose the grandeur of poetic strife.

Chest rose

The thorns, the rose in your chest,
gouged bleeding holes in my flesh.

Her touch

Her velvet touch is the morphine,
to the cancer in my soul's ravine.

Firefly

I'm a firefly,
fluttering in darkness.
Catching eyes,
alleviating people of their loneliness.

Ricin tongues

Ricin laced tongues seeking to ensnare me,
forgetting the immunity of biological crazy.

I envy

I envy those,
made of other materials.
Flexible as cotton fiber clothes,
where I am iron forged ideals.

To my advantage,
on how I am furnace refined.
Cotton vaporizes to dust with age,
iron firmly stands against time.

Tar abyss

The tar abyss,
a scene of eloquence.
With Galactic depth,
monsters made by my penmanship.

Chemical imbalance

Once a Casanova,
words exploding like a supernova.
Chemical imbalance a tedious chore,
society can't realize it just as before.

Present anxiety

Debilitated eyes,
scarred hands.
Scribing lines.
Hourglass sand.

Grains pacing,
Insomnia kicking.
Subconscious racing.
Anxiety striking.

Masochist

Carved into flesh by masochistic tendencies.
Pain was a teacher, yet a delicacy.

Cinder

You brag of cinder,
how dazzling you burn.

One day you'll lose kindling,
spluttering and fading internally.

While I, a creature made of dark,
will continue on even after I part.

My home

My home is in the deciduous twilight forests,
a thousand-mile trek north where the world ignores us.
Shadows falling in channels out of the dwindling rays,
where the people age away but the scenery never changes.

Suppressing depression

Suppressing the regression into depression,
reality is testing this creature of duality.

Manic hours

Lyrically insane in the membrane,
ink flowing deep from within my veins.
Cursed by pain to take a notion to write these verses,
when an ocean of times I should have been in a hearse.

Wish I could say that my words were solar-powered,
but I'm fueled by the gasoline of manic hours.

A fiend

Hands swinging downward on a child like a blacksmith's hammer,
long sleeves in the crimson blistering summer heat to hide bruises.
Tears bringing lead raindrops the size of fists, leading to a stammer,
a small child being dealt a hand of cards from a stacked deck to lose.

Back lashed by a roman legionnaire higher than Mount Arafat on hashish,
arms twisted into a shield to save the face from the bludgeoning.
Legs shaking, the sound of school bells signaling a return to the beast,
hands shivering, chest palpitating at the prospect of a door opening.

Lies leaked into ears from a virgin lambs tongue to hide trauma,
perpetuating the tapestry of violence that wove its threads together.
Unfolding before the globe like a Greek tragedy filled with drama,
a sun irradiated through sky blue, yet eternity was black cloud weather.

Etched in the stone of my mind of monsters and where they descend,
demons require a circle with an incantation easily hidden under a bed.
Poltergeists infest homes, yet, both banes can be banished in the end,
this particular fiend drilled his way into my brain to live on in my head.

The diagnosis

Plutonian raindrops fell down in the season of death,
the frigid wind blowing over the resting mountains and hills.
The dirt on its way to frosting over from winter's breath,
with a child missing from the glass of a dilapidated window sill.

Temperature dropping faster than the descent into Helheim,
ice begins glazing over tar, glossing hardwoods and evergreens.
Taking sullen fields of long since passed grass to be stuck where fell,
feet logged by November's water with a mouth stretched to scream.

Turning to dusk on arms stitched together by needle and thread,
a child's brain was placed upon a scale of old found to be restricted.
The precipice of self-loathing; blood-stained sheets of dread,
steam rising from a fire that lingers as embers flickering.

With a child missing from the view of the glass pane of the sill,
using the bitter rain of winter's chill to numb a wound on the hill.

Modern day Caesar

Ichor soaked clothes turning white to rose,
knives, some of which were never pulled out.
Flesh healed around them in emperor robes,
leaned forward on a throne with a garland of doubt.

Crown seated firmly upon bruised forehead and temples,
hands resting as if dead with calloused knuckles.
A king of the poor in the heart of the new Rome empire,
feet poised to get on the grind while he tightens the buckle.

Rising from the iron seat as darkness sets the stage,
the shocked eyes of the treacherous opening wide with surprise.
Revenge isn't sought; instead, a smirk emblazons their rage,
thighs quivering weakly as lips part the universe of lies.

Not one deathly blow was struck by a well-armed enemy,
the modern-day Caesar was stabbed by all who claimed to love thee.

Acme, TX

On the tar laden path of two-eighty-seven in open fields,
rests a town that tried to dig in its Texas-sized heels.
Surrounded by the waist-high weeds is a starving creation,
a boomtown that vaporized along with its only occupation.

Highway signs of peridot and snow say a population of fourteen,
a place where people saw a contract written like gold from a queen.
The watering hole filled the bucket with money from business,
Acme Texas, a place of gypsum; plaster struck down with a sickness.

Now a phantom town with the plug long since pulled on support,
as buildings made of cedar and oak break down and contort.
All of the steel structures laying down into nothing but rust,
as the town got vaporized into a cloud of gypsum dust.

A deathly hollow of what used to be a pulsing market square,
should have put glasses to the fine print to see the deal was fair.

Idol of mania

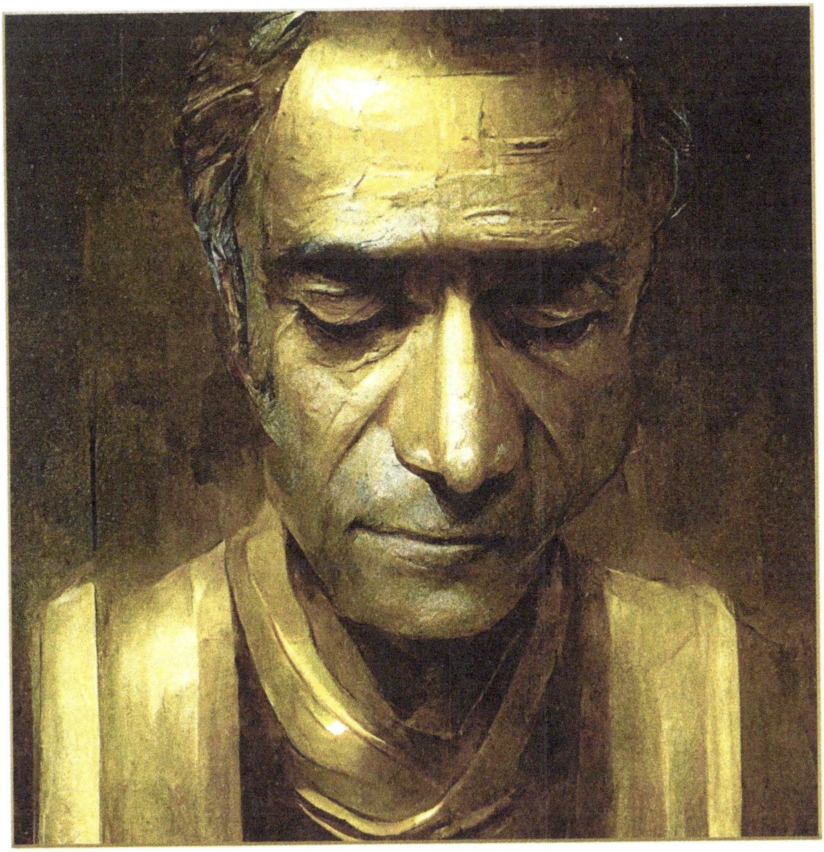

Mild black Earl Grey in a mug when you were craving espresso,
'twas thine forked tongue that flicked sound waves of my divinity.
My feet were illustrious polished brass with hair ethereally pressed,
burning brightly like all the stars above the sinners of the city.

An inspiration that brought perspiration at every inhalation,
eyes giving closer inspection recoiling in ire filled vexation.
While toiling in the strands of heavy burning light for ambitions,
the rope-tied inhibitions broke loose to a finger accusing damnation.

My accusers, who was it that placed me on a pedestal of idolatry?
Recall the call to worship the golden calf of my accomplishments.
Zealous worship of one you praised as though his lips parted the sea,
mirrors crack under a mountainous weight of malicious intent.

Even in the panic of manic expression, I sequestered digression,
claiming to be black mild Earl Grey tea while you craved espresso.
Singing hymns of sainthood then painting me as Mephistopheles,
a deluded twisted frame of conjecture that I never expressed.

Cursed under your venomous vapor breaths in this land,
do not lie, do not contrive, I am as I've always said; just a man.

Intentions

Question your investments,
the best of intentions,
oft turn ladders of ascension,
into churning spirals of a prison dimension.

Suspended in boiling waters,
turning the brain to poison thoughts.
Essence in a Venus fly trap forever caught,
strangling tighter over glitter sought.

Barbed wire digging deeper into flesh,
anxiety using its ribbons to make a nest.
An ambiguous prion coming to infest,
eating the membrane of the sane at rest.

Query the cobblestone that the feet walk,
meditate long before you begin to talk.
Actions have consequences not always outlined in chalk,
your intent well-meant may actually be the jagged rock.

The fireside sin

Crimson red glowing iron in the frostbitten night air of February,
lyrics of moons past through decades of consummate bitter stings.
Whiskey drained bottles lining a breakfast bar bring to mind a story,
a mourning allegory of self-affliction by razors; knives to a pseudonym.

A creature of metal hammered into shape by the flaming swings,
no mold was crafted out of oak or concrete to cast the frame.
Sparks flew into the air from the strikes of a queen with a void king,
the woman with her calloused hands smithed a son with his name.

Though that queen has turned into ash not scattered by the wind,
the child of glowing iron in the shade of an amber sunset remains.
Conceived by the fireside by two in a weathered dimly lit inn,
now a man of glowing iron caught by the death of the void king in pain.

Both the void king and warm loving queen fell into mere dust,
a prince of iron left behind that refuses to stop glowing and turn into rust.

Duality

Fire twisted into spires surrounded by hail smoldering in brimstone,
a sulfur-rich concoction feeding the pyre staving off black sludge.
Burning and consuming as it reaches out of the tar pit alone,
spraying cinders as it expands inhaling oxygen until it trudges.

The cornerstone of flame spluttering and fading as it snuffs out,
the sea of toxic ooze capturing the source of the bright ignition.
The glorious yellow of a burning star turned into a black hole of doubt,
mountain like heavy phantom hands ripping the brain into fission.

A coin resting on its edge at the mercy of the wind blowing,
tapestry-woven neural chemicals fluttering upon the air.
Vacuumed into a machine crocheting and cross-stitching,
designing the directions of the fall of a coin and how my mind fairs.

In the nowhere

A plain of archaic black and white circled by great walls,
shrinking to eye level as feet traverse the flawless white concrete.
Now a ledge of mortar to the view of its beholder stalling,
nose pointing down over the edge to a glow of color streaming.

Whipping around like a turntable with a record of silence,
the rooftop with no doors and no stairs; no stars resting above.
Arms planting onto the ledge to the only sight a mote of essence,
four mighty oaks holding up a blank building above the water hovering.

An ocean made of liquid rainbows feeding the fibrous roots,
extending farther and wider than perception will allow.
The face now a contortionist putting on a show in mute,
to a painting in aqueous canvas that furrows the brow.

A dimension outside of somewhere,
yet cloud height above in the nowhere.

Fae Wood

Sugar; silver and red maples surround a child in the afternoon light,
the air was still as if it had been nailed down by supernal hands.
No songs reverberated from the birds sitting in the trees in sight,
a blight of silence breeding curiosity like rabbits on the mountain strand.

Feet traced over multiple acres of wood with berries and fauna,
peace eventually washed over the boy like a warm day at the seashore.
Teaberry leaves shimmering in the densely amber ray filled sauna,
senses hitting the young man as he turned heels from the forest's core.

Drowsy from the walking eventually trudging to the line of hardwood,
the light was still flowing like a river of radiation showing no signs of slowing.
Breaking the tree line as the boys' eyes grew as wide as where he stood,
day hard shifted into the night without a trace of light left glowing.

Mother with all immediate family strung along with police on loudspeakers,
his tongue and mouth welded shut as he now finally understood.
Left eye twitching slowly, head turning to look toward a giggle that squeaked,
he was never in his grandfather's acres of mixed soft and hardwood.

Manic meltdown

A
raging caged fire,
inside of a trash compactor,
misinterpreted ire staging for a fast multiplication factor.
Sending forty-five caliber-sized drops of sweat,
shooting down the side of a neck for an obvious train wreck.
Hands shaking and quaking with neural chemicals taking,

forsaking sleep having gone too deep into the plutonium filled manic lake.
Drowning in water well known all the way down to the bone,
fraying into radioactive decay branching off of chromosomes.

A lyricist,
recidivism into whiskey,
sipping to keep me asleep.
Knee-deep in muddy misery,
with a noose tied to a tree.
Suffocating in either direction
stretching my midsection,
people acting as advocates of the devil's chosen.
Pretending to be sending hope while shortening the rope,
tongues with words like vending machines placing a price to cope.
Turning purple hurting in the blighted sight of their sound,
appearing to be on the ground but stuck in a manic meltdown.

Dispelling darkness

Bubbling black tar oozing from an open sepulcher,
bubbles pop and splash spreading inherent darkness.
People rush to run away from the spreading incursion,
the black eating away what the light touches, a man harkens.

Quill in hand scribing lines from scarred olive hands,
the crowd quivers behind the one left behind them.
Toxic ooze soaked up by papyrus colored similar to sand,
forming words on pages as concrete castles in the frost of autumn.

In the tars place springs up shooting timber and flowers,
fields of flowers bloom upon the once desecrated soil.
Sludge polluted rivers wiped crystal clear in the hour,
air lingering with a scent easily picked up by the nose of floral oils.

The crowd amazed at the acrobatics to pull this stunt,
a man treading the plane of green in ragged clothes popping out so stark.
Words flowing out aqueous of inspiration and loving the descriptive hunt,
laying the pages of how he was dispelling the darkness.

Poison

Wolfsbane soaked knives aimed at the backs of enemies
tongues dripping with the intoxicatingly sweet venom.
Chalice cups filled with pressed wine mixed with ricin,
Iliad's filled with glorious stories of treachery enticing.

Most of us though are Socrates and our hemlock tea,
sipping heart halting mixtures in our temporal glory.
Contained in the mugs we choose to display outwardly,
pride stretches out, rising like a flame into a spout.

Words of Solomon couldn't penetrate our diamond hides,
dipping into the grain alcohol worlds where we reside.
Falling into people, coal lining their imaginations as they're seething,
thickening the air into iron clay with a smile entreating.

Their razor blade tongues lacerating making the blood flow,
their lips deceivingly pursued like Egyptian cotton pillows.
Arms stretched open wide, casting lots against you,
voices echoing off the atmosphere of poisons we choose.

Suicide

Scars painted over a stretched out canvas of a young body,
self-affliction of knives and razors long since faded to shadows.
A canvas painted out in brushstrokes lacquered by actions of acidic thoughts,
thoughts that bubbled their way through the paper-thin resolve of a dim glow.

Mirages filled with watery voices calling for the slicing of flesh,
gurgling through a veil of dark particles floating in the still air.
Calling for the sight of blood-red iron falling to the floor to rest,
iron maidens draining every drop, seemingly to propose a solution fair.

Flogging and flaying of sinew to the bone offers more on the scales,
draining soft rose into bleached skin is the only logical choice.
Like a keg in a tap draining away the mystery of the darkened veil,
the razor's edge cutting and trailblazing a path to no thought or voice.

Wisdom carved into the granite, remarking on sanity clearly,
Vantablack anguish might be eating you like a spirit of gluttony.
Yet bitter tear streams will cloud the rooms in their misery,
flooding the rooms where you grew up and used to be.

Gouging out ichor making the floor thicker will never answer why,
electrical pulses, logic will define why the answer was never suicide.

Bloom in darkness

I am a Martian in a marshland in the southeast land of trees,
a weed transplanted into the soil from a thousand miles away.
Taking root into the earth where I've been burned and spurned,
churned into the dirt, my roots made me sprout back up into the fray.

My leaves and vines twisting around the rugged oaks climbing,
dining on the rays of blazing golden sunlight from beyond sight.
Tasting with my tongue iron and water to keep track of the time,
spreading out in lush peridot green though some call me blight.

My flowers of royal blue growing above the canopy of trees,
the ravens and crows collect me implicitly if you look and harken.
Others who grow spread their pollen at sunrise when they feel free,
with the tide and the moon rising on the horizon I bloom in darkness.

Survivors' remorse

Nostalgia a megaton blast to the stomach causing a wretch,
the sting of regret like a scorpion strike to the brain.
Venom injected into the neural globe of a subconscious stretch,
a young girl in an open sepulcher getting ready to be laid in vain.

A brown haired girl with eyes of sparkling green emerald gems,
still as a tomb on the eve of its closure never to have its air stirred.
A girl who scribbled in notebooks for a boy who didn't notice them,
razor blades ended a charade of happiness for the girl.

Many moons have passed and many new bright-lit days come,
the hourglass of my time still seems to keep draining on.
Yet the memory thereof still keeps pressing down with its thumb,
with gravity like Jupiter ripping my essence, wondering if I'll succumb.

The memory of a young girl and a young boy haunts my dreams,
wondering if I'd known if I could have restitched fate to a different seam.

The rain

The rain driving sideways drenching everything in sight,
dragging down like a brass anchor cutting through the depths.
Bullets of rain raining down as day turns into a tea steeped night,
cutting the surface of the earth from the sky that wept.

Soon a deluge of rancid thoughts clawing like crazed beasts,
rising up through the floorboards soaking the feet of those who walk.
Water burning like a fire ripping through the canopy of trees,
layering up as bricks being laid almost all the way to where you talk.

Even then though the rain has to persist until seas exist,
swim until your feet trudge the very bottom of the shore.
See that you're standing again, there is no reason to be a recidivist,
this is a tropical paradise laid out with fruits never seen before.

Even if you don't believe that you can possibly get there,
it's just a little rain sprinkling down all around, a little misting.
Just a drop or two of dew into a downpour ensnaring,
it doesn't mean you're physically weak, you're strong I insist.

It's ok to cry and let the floodgates open I hope you know,
for without the rain hammering down, how could anything grow?

Wisdom splinters

Long winding roads weaved together like a wicker basket,
gravel stretching like the horizon filled with potholes and bumps.
Tripping and falling on grand stumbling blocks of granite,
cuts gouging into flesh like railroad spikes hammered thump by thump.

Coughing up red ichor into napkins from the internal bleeding,
running out of wind as your energy rescinds into the entropy.
Pages stuck together refusing to turn to the diamond learned reading,
a body stitched down to the soil, pinned down in inertia developing.

Twenty-eight years of lessons bludgeoning like aluminum bats,
hard-earned scars laid out as hides of animals from Siberian winters.
Quivering from the frigid cold calculator of ice-laden facts,
staying warm by the light of kidding, set ablaze from wisdom splinters.

Made of iron

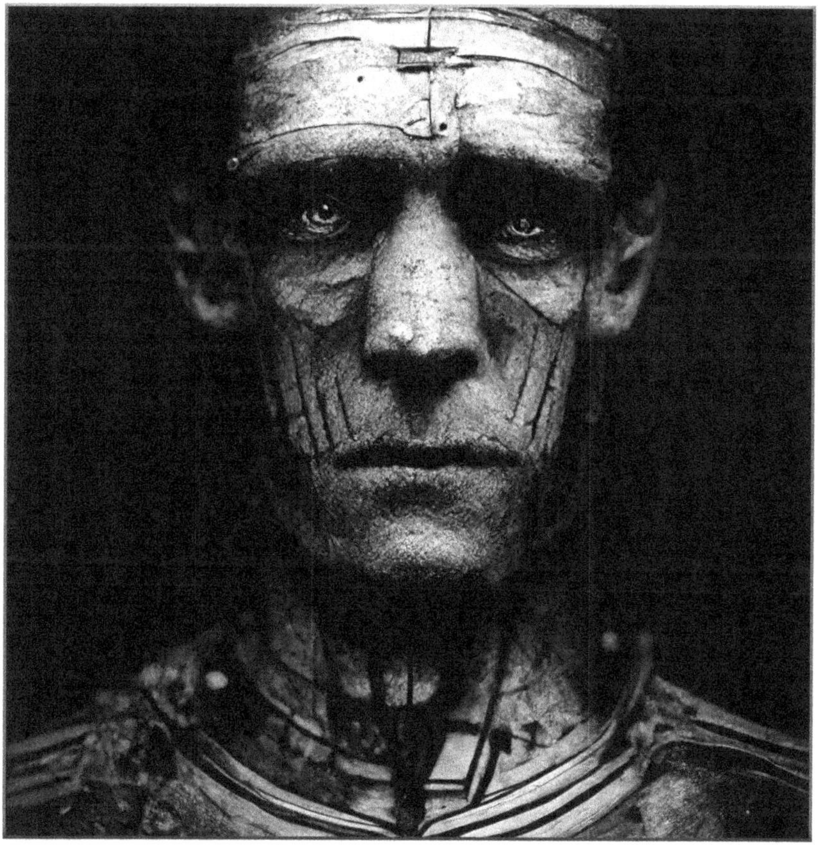

People are made out of different elements of the world we live in,
I myself am iron cast before flames that harden and blacken.
Once tempered and polished into a dull mirror oxidizing and rusting,
iron bears monstrous loads getting stacked like wood before the oven.

Iron can be forged into weapons of war or stretchers of healing,
smelted and poured into forms for tools to go out and work the world.
It can be shaped into beams that support the cave in of the ceiling,
swinging back at the elements as the strikes begin to be hurled.

Being a little marble piece of iron in a world made of a pyre,
tossed through the air dragged down by gravity into the water.
Pushed by underwater currents back to the earth that feeds the fire,
Turned orange by the strike of lightning acting as an igniter.

Sometimes it feels like blood-soaked conflict and I'm being fired upon,
in this uncertain globe, I don't regret being made of iron.

Grand thoughts

Tingling electricity floating over the horizon of the skin,
raising hairs like magicians to hypodermic needle points.
Charging cells with euphoric static crawling by pins,
the vise loosening its grip on the appointed impulse joints.

Gravity becoming as fluffy as sugar clouds of strawberry,
every syllable rolling off the tongue like chocolate malted milk balls.
A morphine dream of feather light resistance to actions cause,
firing Gatling gun streams of lead while the wagon heads to fall.

Water colored dreams within the hands grasping reach,
fingertips grazing against the blue sapphire encrusted crown.
The floorboards rippling under the toe as water comes to bleach,
staring at rainbow stained hands on the bullet fall down.

Air whizzing through the hair on the descent to rock bottom,
smacking the frigid steel floor at the end of grand thoughts.

Skittering madness

Holes lined as a battle zone of craters billowing the smolder,
erratically sewn together to start breeding tissues into scars.
Wounds cut into fresh blood, while some have leathered over.
self-affliction ringing bells through the snowfall like a shooting star.

A memory of fog hiding etched tablets blanketed by oil-thick mist,
the echoes of scattered footsteps chiming like coins being dropped.
Flashes of memories striking like a cobra that never made a hiss,
pumping venom to the clouds, an apricated green tint soaking thoughts.

Stirring into spirals from mouse stepping through poison haze,
stumbling into a run to escape the tar thick gaseous venom pit.
As the light floods through an opening in the cobblestone archway,
snapping like a bone back into the crystal clean air of reality.

Shoulders shuddering to a faint giggle at the back of a dangerous mind,
glacial fingers trailing the curvature of the spine to a bitter chill.
The darkness of the mortal coil being compressed into a liquid inside,
draining into ink being absorbed on bleached white paper hills.

A collection of pages with words that were darkly harnessed,
showing in black and white my monsters of skittering madness.

Dark rider

Cloaked in leather and denim with a hood of a faded canvas,
bouncing to the trot of a horse going through the wilderness.
Black clouds follow in step not far behind over the landmass,
as the stout dark gaunt rider dismounts at the gray inn for rest.

Grabbing the leather-bound book lined by silver from the saddlebag,
stepping through the pine sap lacquered door to patrons in a gloom.
Opening up the black tome and picking a rough oak chair to straddle,
the syllables echo as the book returns color from darkened doom.

As the rain begins to pour like an open faucet on the outside,
hammering the soil like a jackhammer into a worn-out concrete.
Leaving the speechless to go stable a horse away from the cloud,
strapping a food bag to be disturbed by an untimely squeak.

A man in tears at the relief asking, "Who are you, mister?"
Crow's feet wrinkled up on one side to the half of a smirk.
Without turning to him he responded in a hoarse voice insisting,
"I'm just a dark rider out on the range who has unfinished work."

Boxing match (a PTSD poem)

The echo of a bell chime coming through the mud slurry thick air,
drenched by the rainfall of perspiration of a rock wall defense.
Another round of brain cinema is up to trigger a snare,
entangling you in a silk web where all it needs is patience.

Another volley of pain falling down like arrows once again,
with every arrow tracing its way into the main memory vein.
Gravity driving them deeper like divers searching for Atlantis,
meanwhile, the body is dirty dancing to the rhythm of pain.

Another bell ring zipping through dry heaving and heavy breathing,
as vomit gets coughed up onto the dilapidated boxing ring floor.
How many rounds have gone down since the beginning of the grieving,
how many more bludgeoning blows must come raining on the core?

Times up with more left hooks and jabs straight into the cerebrum,
guards get put up but depression is creeping through the window.
Two phantom grizzly bears to fight off now in a place beyond the sun,
defense breaking into shaking as it starts to seem to crescendo.

Another round is up in the bleary-eyed sight,
Superman standing before his fatal kryptonite.
Turmoil circling the incandescent lights,
dig deep, and keep up the fight.

My soul

Diamonds fitted as studs into high karat golden rings,
chrome rims adorned by the modern-day painted chariots.
Integrity sold at auction to the highest bidder singing,
feigning over thirty pieces of silver like Judas Iscariot.

Paintings and songs just another notch on a bedpost,
cinema appearances on the grand stage of the old silver screen.
Silver and gold pouring like rivers touched by king Midas's ghost,
with the rising volcanic mountain of stress building a scream.

Many people come peddling tales of success and renown,
showcasing the cashmere lies in an Italian leather wallet.
Slips of paper printed with phrases that are godly sounding,
little pieces of green hooked on to a fishing line that is calling.

Still viewing the world through a nineties vintage lens,
I haven't the tinkling change for that road with its toll.
Though I might run into many walls, I'll never be on the fence,
deals bonded in deceit and ink are not worth the lucre of my soul.

My razor-edged tongue

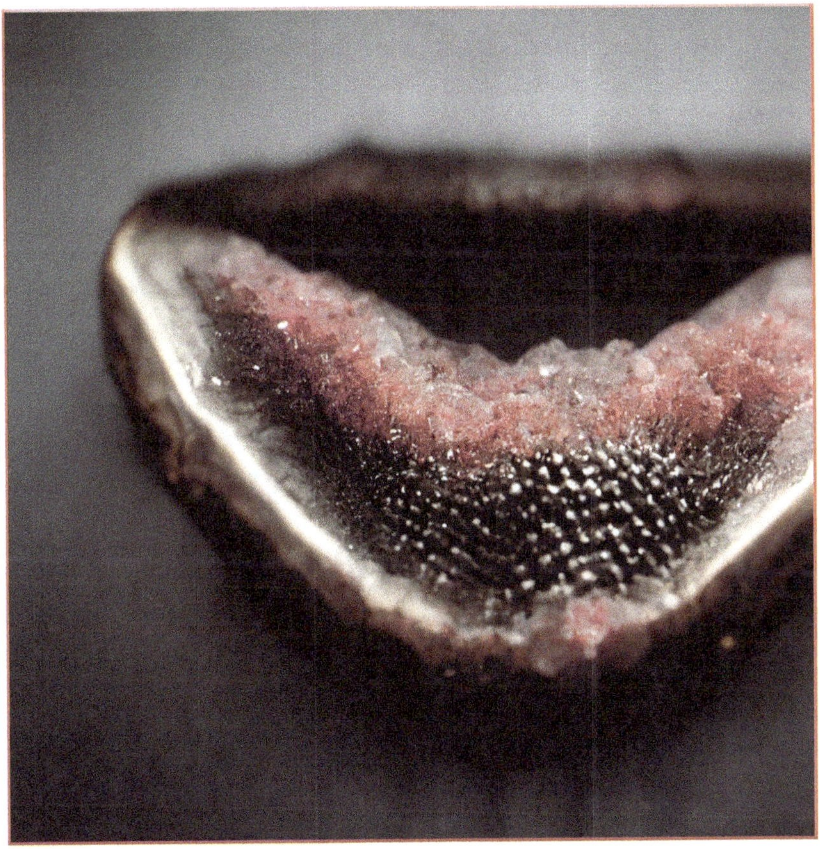

My razor-edged tongue carved wounds,
like a rapier that carved initials into trees.
A sword leading others to their tombs,
casting a rain of misery soaking them freely.

The words were boiling hot slags and magma,
steel ire nailed into the meek and unsuspecting.
Slashing and burning the hearts of those who stagger,
jaggedly hollowing out people like jack o lanterns for inspection.

Grains of sand falling through the middle of the hourglass,
granules of mercy raining down for the chance to atone.
Grabbing a handful of sand to rub with all my earthly power,
grinding with shaky tendons vibrating on the hone.

Dismantling that megaton nuclear bomb that would rain fire,
reforging it into a quill to scribe tales of the flaming spire.
Poetic strife remains like a sermon to the choir,
muscles move mysteriously to lift others higher.

Apple of darkness

On a faux marble countertop lays a vivacious red apple,
reflecting strands of light thin as the hair of the elderly.
Flowing from it like a slow-motion waterfall of black sap,
wisps of dark mist floating like feathers to the floor to be held.

Covering the sky blue ceramic floor like dandelion seedlings,
vapor climbing walls like rock climbers on a mountain trek.
Slipping through the sieve of a screen door calling out to feed,
whispering tales of jet black wisdom at the napes of necks.

Calling for the bludgeoned, the betrayed, and the craven,
somber words spiraling like tornadoes into curious ears.
An obsidian glow weighed on scales as a raven,
yet tender fleshed with sweet juices to cast out fear.

Follow the billow to the ambrosia of greatness,
take a bite and learn from my pulsing apple of darkness.

Darkness wasn't the end

Carbon steel piercing into an olive shoulder,
slicing through and sliding over the bone.
Carving living clay that pulsed out mud coldly,
clogging in the open well long before the ride home.

Whispering wind, blowing into the ears of a mother,
a fire pushing past the tear-shaped heart, breaking.
Throwing warm hug words to someone suffering,
a black-robed figure riding in for a hostage taking.

A void father, septic going into a lightning shock,
a scream cutting through like coyotes into the night.
Snow flaking down against the hands of the clock,
limping after one thousand miles slowly drifting out of sight.

Wounds stacked up like cards in a rigged deck,
dealt round after round trying to beat the madness descending.
Nerve damage tingling down the back through the neck,
thoughts smashing in like a murderer through the walls rendering.

Thoughts now mumble off about a life intestinally rending,
stars dot the night spelling out darkness wasn't the end.

Ragnarok

An iron grip wrenching into a brass spear that never misses,
blood dribbling down a forest of hair sewn into a leather face.
Two ravens circling gaunt charcoal skies seeking out fissures,
their perch on rugged granite shoulders that have fallen from pace.

Whispering lead secrets to the father of blood stained sacrifice,
as marble hearth begins to shake all the way down to the Bifrost.
The frigid wind of fate snaking through the cracks with its touch of ice,
thunder cracks in the distance with the echo of bloodshed's cost.

Fire erupting like abscesses from deep inside the soil of Asgard,
as the wolves growl is not the only thundering sound on the horizon.
Ancient ivory bones sink like an anchor into a sea of bismuth hardness,
after and forethought chirping in the ears of the one eyed one.

Rising like a tsunami from the throne to a kingdom crying out,
time to put the myth of fate to bed like a haughty child.
Through the black marble archway fire rains down with smoke clouds,
a giant of magma drenching Valkyries in flame from the west wilds.

A wolf snarls from halfway down the royal steps with ire,
charging and clamping down its voracious jaws into Aesir flesh.
Gouging a spear into the beastly eye, ending a feud that's tired,
veins dangling from the rends of fangs into a crimson mess.

Ravens disperse upwards with blood on their wings into steam,
when they land again, the realm will know what it means.

Dust

Noxious dust solidifying into still motion pictures,
the sun burning brighter as the world seems to rust.
Dulling into a snow fall blur of a fourth dimension rift,
every taste of sweet and bitter, the same as a case of thrush.

Waking moments a time loop of questions that never cease,
raking the walls of the brain like railroad spikes on a chalkboard.
A venomous guilt sinking in its injections that never ease,
carving strips of insanity out like dried meat to be hoarded.

Salt water droplets unable to rehydrate and reanimate,
plowing through the valleys of a face turned toward the past.
Toward the sunny field of dreams that rot into an alum reality,
puckering the hippocampus with lines of flayed lashes.

Breathing like double pneumonia caught in a sea fog,
regret trickling in like drought ridden streams heat hushed.
Heart pounding like Thor's hammer against the serpent in the bog,
the world blown by a glassblower with no flame, just dust.

Fighter

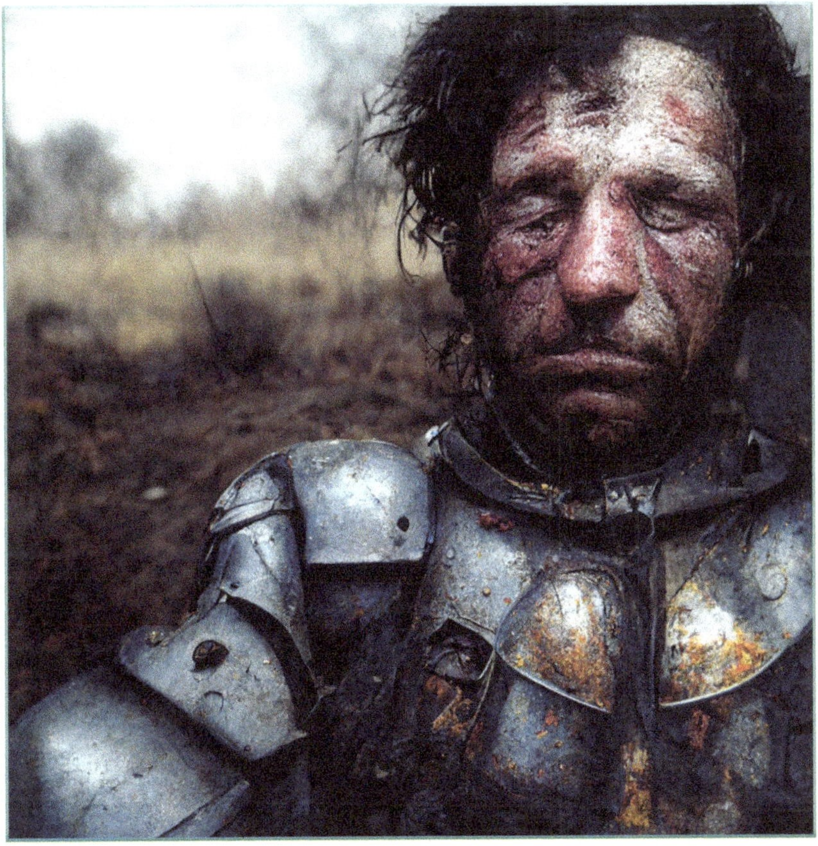

Blades punching into flesh, fists painting skin black and blue,
eye line a sunset of color after the struggle of muscles.
Day old blood spat out of a mouth from someone who never knew,
the scales weighing the value of silence over the hustle.

Striking like a snake at any passerby who dare approach,
coiling and strangling anything that stood between resources.
Starving thoughts like outer space freezing any reproach,
bits of paper with deceased faces trickled instead of coursing.

Hammer striking nails into the preserve soaked pine wood,
sweat pouring like the rain down a forehead to the echo of thunder.
A storm brewing above like a French press where the work stood,
lightning cracking like a titans whip to push the earth asunder.

Voices radiating through underneath a motionless gray sky,
grasping at the smooth stone reinforced focus for resources.
Rain shrouding the tears that were covered up by lies,
as bits of paper with deceased faces trickled but never coursed.

Ashes sifting through young labor worn hands,
Rome was built and burnt at the hands of a fighter.
Love starved thoughts burning like Pompeii sand,
the scales weighing the value of a lover over the fighter.

Reaching like a ladder of hope at any passerby who dare approach,
the typhoon of sorrow siphoning out all of the resources.
Yet even if the earth spun backwards without time to reproach,
to where the hourglass would flip and begin again from the source.

Fate would not undo its chisel to the stone through endless nights,
leaving me yet again on the scale with my weight as a fighter.

King of the north

Frozen tears cascading down toward a glass chalice,
floating in the sway of Gaia's breath in a painting of autumn.
Clouds worming their way through nostrils flared with malice,
concrete gray skies lining the orange peel trees under frost's thumb.

Ravens swirling charcoaled fields like a storm on a turntable,
landing like darts on a board billowing with smoke and ember.
The ice embracing the fire like a dance between lovers in a fable,
a glare pierces the south as time marches on into December.

Iron and stone hewn together like the bread from a bakers oven,
along the walls, a granite man with leathered hands of patience.
Standing as a redwood in a clear cut plain looking at the horizon,
snarling as the words write curses in the air to be tainted.

Night falls like an eyelid closing for the ethereal world of dreams,
yet one set of eyes refuse to fall into the realm of the source.
Heated by ire that flows through the veins like Nordic streams,
a balled fist rests on a pommel of an ax from the king of the north.

Die trying

A heart like a sponge in the liquid burn of whiskey,
fire crawling through the veins and taking a seat in the brain.
Morphine dripping into the murky lake of the pneumas misery,
no pillow, no cotton breast to rest upon from the stimulant of pain.

Sipping down the circling calico colors of joy from a dollar stein,
darkness and land, the separating obsidian veil from home.
The ground attacks the feet with blisters and no lucre to find,
a noose hanging satchel empty of gold from where they roam.

The harp of destiny echoes through the fog of living,
a fingertip's reach off from the strings to be plucked.
Where the coal-stained clouds leak like a sieve,
lightning striking like a predator at the drip drops of luck.

Raking with crimson digits silver maple wood into a bow,
raw shaking palms pulling back the stem of an arrow.
Whipping from the crack of the string in a ghastly glow,
snapping the suspended harp as it falls in tow.

Frothing at the mouth as the body falls like a crippled tower,
crawling through a seizure from cosmic radiation like vying.
One grimaced swipe at a time forward from the waning power,
full throttle decay or not they'd rather die trying.

Smiled like I meant it

Eyes tracing the shadows in the onyx lake of the abyss,
rising like flames, embracing like an old friend on leave from the foyer.
Corners of a mouth stretching into a half-moon smile so crisp,
those same eyes, a dam holding back the tides so coy.

Stings, lacerations and bruises as the corners stayed pinned tight,
cherry blossom red lips never quivering to the slings and arrows.
Lips that lost their color through a river of blood out of sight,
no tourniquet to cut and polish the eyes that used to glow.

Sky blue and purple mistakes littering a beating muscle,
releasing its flood gate of burgundy into a tsunami.
The smile freeze dried and frost burnt in the everyday hustle,
ripping into papier mache and patching the cracks externally.

Brain fissuring into a plutonium mushroom cloud,
as the eyes twitch with the smile in a state of permafrost.
Nuclear destruction came without a cracking of sound,
smiling through the flaying, praying to have enough to pay the cost.

Insomnia madness

Earthquake rattle climbing eggshell walls,
shadows reaching and grabbing in mist.
Cracking and groaning from the breathing halls,
sunlight flickers from a clear sky in the distance.

Slate gray rain blotting out the colors of the day,
time-stained hands of the clock dulled to white.
Globe whipping like cream in a mixer without delay,
sun bursts in the abyss, splintering holes in the night.

Bismuth dreams dripping through the ceiling texture,
molten spots splashing against skin like cigarette embers.
Furniture nails pin cushioning lungs in a Victorian vex,
vapors clouding logic into engine parts to be assembled.

Wisps of phantoms passing through the living room,
clawing with whispers at the ear drums in taps.
Eyes bloodshot from the clashing thoughts of doom,
snapping at outlines of figures in bolo ties and hats.

Wind howling outside windows with trees cracking,
the orange and gold blizzard dancing to the song.
A rhythmic blur where the light and dark swap,
with cackling madness seeping into days gone.

The beast depression

Light begins cracking through the abyssal glass of night,
fracturing like stained glass to be placed in a mural.
Darkness being burned into a vapor memory before the light,
claws reaching and raking, fighting the boiling as its burial.

Rending into the heaving chest as it stretches like elastic
tethering its black octopus limbs around a racing heart.
Suction cups filled with teeth cutting like a picture through static,
Stygian burning touch like ravines of fire miles apart.

Black birds cackling out the echoing sound of a loosening grip,
shreds of flesh vanishing into blood curdling pain.
Rippling like a wave tossing everything to and fro on the ship,
splashing the remnants, fading and leaving a black coffee stain.

Claws scratching against the fall into the crack of the void,
sewing itself closed, cross threading itself in rotation.
Coughing and hacking from the splintering back into joy,
cotton wisps of clouds rolling by as a peaceful sensation.

Cherry smeared across the sky before the stars is a delight,
rouge smudged before the rising fire is a sailors warning.
One that prophesies a kraken to strike in the center of night,
depression the true beast of the sea that all abhor.

Left alone

Black licorice dreams rippling out like molasses,
the locomotive has lost all steam on the tracks.
Fires blown out in a gust with a furnace empty of coal,
gravity blast stacking like a box on top of traction.

A forest deluged in silence beyond echoing voices,
where light fades off into a sphere of nothing.
The embers fading into soot from an engineer's choices,
still air hangs like prisoners of war at the end of struggling.

Signs posted in a wagon circle staving off entrance,
food and drink collecting dust on a pressboard shelf.
A blank stare off into the pastel-colored trees at the advance,
sea of gray faces scratching at the borders for help.

Stiff retreat into the tempered iron shell,
quiet as a mouse and still as a stone.
The echo chamber of voices rattle like chains from hell,
river eyes soaking mountain knees only wanting to be left alone.

Stigma

One word played from the harp of vocal cords,
floating on the air like a leaf lost in the breeze.
Swirling and running away carelessly into the fjord,
to be lost like days of time in the rings of trees.

Soaked by ice laden waters in its swish of foam,
splashed on stone just to be sucked back out to the unknown.
Crushed over and over until it's spat out on its new home,
an emerald green in a sea of sand standing out alone.

Compressed under the weight of sandals and shoes,
driving ever deeper like drops of rain from the storm into soil.
Thinning out from the grinding to be like paper that reads the news,
a domino chain that was whipped forward from an initial recoil.

One word is like shrink wrap clinging to the face,
suffocating like volcanic gasses trailing off of molten magma.
One-word bludgeons like time and a leaf left to its fate,
a word held tightly in the synapses in a state of stagnation.

Never said but always implied like an assassin in disguise,
sorting and filing you away far from touch where you'll lie.

Monster

Fist clenched like a black obsidian cannon ball,
launching into faces like ships on open waters.
Watching masts of men snap into the lead weighted fall,
blood splashing out of mouths, rolling down knuckles in a saunter.

Thirty pieces of silver slapping the worn pine table,
a coin careening off toward the decadent marble tile.
The tinkling chime sending a shudder worthy of a fable,
a crooked walk down a crooked mile with jobs on a crooked stile.

Moons passed over many crocheted fibers of night,
stars rocked back and forth in and out of alignment.
Hands aching and trembling for the easy road of the fight,
with a whetted mind against the churn of iron scent.

Faces blow past like the breeze in a blissful hum,
taking blows dealt out like the deck of fifty-two.
Inscribed in muscles are all of the deeds that have been done,
some tigers do change their stripes, it's true.

Prison stall

Talking to the ornately painted walls,
like I laid the concrete for my prison stall.
watching the screen in a dream of my faults.
Falling deeper in,
the wave on a chain drag of sins,
drowning but the waters only as deep as the kitchen sink.
I get lost in the sauce,
too many things going on.

got people dying while they're trying to see my book.
Pushing against gravities cushion,
into a sight of fighting to get the only thing,
that makes a last wish feel like a fist to the balls.

Kissed with misery,
that's blessed and tested me,
spat in my eye like it didn't respect me.
That's why my nose bleeds,
my eyes feel like they're trying to leave their seats.
But I can't let go,
I've finally got a handle on this show
that seems set in stone,
when I was a child up in the northern wilds I roamed alone,
tree to tree and stone to stone.
Put me in a place to feel like a race I could win,
because I'd never be that lonely again.

Steel toes for breakfast,
mania for lunch and depression for dinner,
ptsd for a midnight snack.
Coming out to attack,
best seat for a treat,
to the cinema.
I'm my own worst enemy,
I can hang me up in villainy
and claim it's an epiphany,
a symphony of destruction
the hum of a black holes suction.
I don't know how to fluctuate and break the chains
the past that has their shiv still into me
like your brain stuck on a melody.

I feel crazy when I'm shuddering in pain,
I race, I pace, I stand and I sit,
I'm thankful for everything that I can get.
But I can't seem to get the meditation to work,
I'm a bottle of coke in a paint shaker on full throttle,
just waiting to be uncorked.
I'm just trying to be the best version of me,
the new download version of two-point-O,
so I can go,
finally look to play a part in the show.
I'm literally dying while trying to be the upgraded version.

Talking to these walls,
my pain is beating me incessantly,
like it's trying to bless me with bruises,
contusions, swelling my brain.
like Alice in wonderland,
when she ate from the wrong porcelain hand.
Is this what better looks like?
in the face of the night,
where the demons creep in.

Why am I blighted by the plight of visions in my sight,
I've perspired long past the point of being tired.
When does surviving turn into thriving,
when can I wash all of the conniving from me?
Do I really need to work until my eyes and ears bleed,
from the stress that's been pressing me down
like a spring ready to fling out.

I've been the strong one my whole life,
if anyone were to kill me somehow I would be guilty.
Sorry, just talking to the walls,
looking out from my prison stall.

Social battery

Questions poised like daggers ready for the thrust,
ripping straight into the core, slicing past the crust.
A razor edge flaying like carved flint rocks,
many different corner stones to bleed out my thoughts.

Soaking in syllables like ink staining a page,
searching a dictionary for the salve to the rage.
Tongue swollen by token placed misery,
hands typing out keystrokes to soothe the history.

Thoughts stretched like rubber into a sling,
hitting marks on targets in a mythical swing.
Veins of cracks from the ripping strain,
swallowing up trains on the tracks of thoughts in the brain.

Climbing mountainous peaks into snow covered caps,
ears clouded by shrieks seeking another fact.
Frozen into a sheet of ice turning away from the matter,
clamoring hands reaching and pulling until I shatter.

Spattered like mud tossed against the glass window,
scales weighing saliva against the trail's foliage.
Flipping past words and the tired footsteps,
into tear-soaked pillows with a social battery in debt.

Suicide hotline

I can't tell you what it feels like,
pressed with a knife in the night.
Phone call in sight with sorrow for us all,
sprawled out like a boxer on the mat,
but no one can see him giving taps.

Stars circling like water for the drain,
high on the memories and pain,
fiending to never feel that way again.

Drenched in tears and sweat,
of hurricanes splash down wet,
a tsunami just leveling the coast.
A kind of fear that can only be found in a ghost.

Sometimes you don't choose,
but you still get chose,
you have to act like it's a fact.
Already rose to the challenge,
like Hercules with a labor to savor,
the bitterness on the tongue.
Knowing that it can either glow up or blow up,
take the time to show up.

Even Atlas was known to shiver under the weight,
muscles quivering under static pressure,
wind blowing by his waist.
Knocking him around with oceans that can drown,
Sweat drops as the tendons pop like firecrackers,
fat cells burning behind the eyes,
not a single face caught in surprise at the sinking demise.

Pistol cocked back with a forty caliber on the tracks,
trying to splatter away all of the shattered glass pain.
Salt spray through two bars underneath the stars,
hands bleeding as muscles rip from the trip,
grabbing a grip on the gravity of stone and dirt.
Lifting away the hurt,
bandaging the thousand cuts,
pulling them from the ruts.

Anxiety

Fire and rain twisting into a spiral of smoke and ash,
sweat pouring like a typhoon caught on the coast.
Soaking in to the hearth of sheets layered behind glass,
hidden in a shadow encrusted room into a black void host.

Lightning anointing itself across skin with arcane magic,
chest rattling like a diesel engine sputtering on empty.
Lungs reaching and grasping and gasping for air in tragedy,
floccose wisps kissing the eyes like a lover so delicately.

A spinning record on an accelerating turntable into a fable,
specters clawing at eardrums mashing the gas pedal to the floor.
Breath inhaled at Mach three speeds losing the grip on stability,
nucleonic fire rising up the spine to critical melt down in the core.

Rocking back forth as a drill carves a hole through the breast,
the black hole stripping flesh out in fibers into gravities grasp.
Baneful snakes constricting like a vise on a tin can in the chest,
choking out the light with a blazing ember filled gasp.

Fading and falling into the cosmos away from the stars,
murmurs trailing off out of reach from the scars.

Self-destructive tendencies

Gluttonous acid rain drops pouring down swallowing up earth,
Lilliputian mouths devouring relationships as their teeth gnaw.
Cutting through chains that bind with a voracious appetite that's cursed,
grinding away the wraps around obsidian pillars as the crow caws.

Injecting the clouds with sulfur mist from the mash of a button,
gently embracing fire as it burns with feet near the edge of oblivion.
Staring down at the hands that drew out words without stuttering,
stained with the ink from the veins smearing out crawling sins.

Plunging down into the clamoring water that the ferryman rides,
snapping back cliff side from the Jupiter pull of a taut rope.
In dark side of the moon applause rises like the turbulent tide,
with the obsidian glass pecked with cracks of their hope.

Tungsten heavy eyes grimaced by the clasp of hands,
pawing and signing relief in the staggering silence.
Carried back to be laid upon gritty cushioning of sand,
nitroglycerin with the reflection as the target of violence.

Ransom

Fire crackling from fat-soaked cloth with embers fraying,
twisting and dancing in the breeze to the drop of sackcloth.
Splintering against the ebony hands wrapped up praying,
coating all in the dew of tar dripping down to light loss.

A sphere lacking a single thread of light to poke through,
feet soaked in jet black, sucking out the color of life.
Sinking by each footstep into the maw of abyssal soup,
pulling like hands of hades with calf deep strife.

Walking in tune with the drops of oil showering down,
feet tracing a line of steps through the slicks of gravel.
Floating above the mire to an exhausted ready to drown,
picking up the torch from the stranger in a grovel.

Striking a pose to toss a flame into the line of trees,
watching the ignition flare up into an open sea of fire.
Dragging at first and carrying second to the clear vicinity,
flames kissing the back of heels into glen out of the mire.

Panting and coughing out soot from the realm of other,
a small price to pay for ransom from darkness for a sister or brother.

Chains

Frigid iron wrapping around forearms like metallic lace,
weaved together in a chain mail pattern leaving the bruised face.
Orange streaks against skin brushed on from the links of a leash,
pitted from the air blowing by with rain and then the sun with its heat.

Brittle rattles in the frost as the seasons turn the page,
lines of sewn together metal showcasing a tension-built cage.
Strung like a fishing net anchored down with lead at the fringes,
tugging an unfamiliar sound burns against the silence in a singe.

Earthbound chains clattering to the ground in clouds of dust,
whipped away by the wind from a baleful gust.
The spirits of chains lingering at the obsidian of dusk,
remnants remain as outlines etched in rust.

Shadows of the stings that once were,
restraining phantoms that were seen but never heard.
As not a single eye stirs when one is breaking free,
memories will never drop a silver screen to show the scenes.

Be it for a thunder of applause rallying your might,
striking out with viper snaps for the lust of the fight.,
Grab a fist full of chains to pull down your post,
until you've fought so much that the chains become ghosts.

Hope

Rusted shut metal hinges stacked atop dry rotted oak,
dank dark room of rose granite with nary a brazier.
No golden glow radiating off the walls of a fire stoked,
footsteps a distant echo rattling from inside the cage.

Monsters clawing against ragged stone with a screech,
grating against the outside like a cat on a scratch post.
Rocks tumbling off to be pounded into a sandy beach,
battering rams cracking through the blocks to get close.

Heaving against inertia, lungs dashing away breath,
muscles screaming from a raging fire consuming them.
Pulling transforming into punches from the east to west,
shaking as it lifted the chest lid filled with nothing inside the den.

Grinding suddenly drowning out to a newfound silence,
banging and crumbling walking further into nothing.
A fortress no longer under siege from the blood-soaked violence,
sweat drops replaced by confusion of an eye on a barren something.

Walking and tripping down the shadow filled corridor,
tremors no longer quaking the walkway suspended with rope.
Bloodthirsty warriors threw down their swords,
realizing the captive had unlocked hope.

You're not alone

A heartbreaking off under a chisel like quarried stone,
crumbling like a sandcastle caught under the next wave.
Petrified by a gaze of medusa as you stare off into the abyss alone,
its black web grabbing and tarnishing your brilliant flame.

Droplets from the eyes flowing like rivers through the mountain pass,
crashing like meteors into the atmosphere with the eruption of fire.
Consumed by the threads of smoke weaving rage fastidious,
smoldering charcoal with cinders popping the glowing orange ire.

Standing like an oak atop the desiccated sand perch of a mound,
looking at the barren graying field of dust filled emptiness.
Shivering under the shrill bitter wind lacerating with its sound,
plunging deep like a diver into the frozen sea.

Railing yourself with a nail studded whip of overanalyzed sins,
ripping out your wrongdoing one flay at time trying to atone.
Kick your legs into a sprint my most beloved of kin,
grab tight, you're not alone.

Missing person's report

I sat there waiting patiently at the bar like a bird in a perch as if its meal ticket was going to show up at any moment, exhaling from a long drag off of a smoke. I had to admit that I looked more like someone who would be basking in the glow of a trash can fire rather than to be seated at the bar with a double shot of crown royal sitting neat in its glass. Then again, what would you expect out of someone who got woken up at three a.m. over a phone call that made as much sense as trying to find the philosophers' stone in a modern-day world. She was on the other end of the phone too frantic to even attempt at making an entirely coherent sentence, let alone be driving up to the only bar in town that stayed open all night. My weary eyes traced the outside of my glass, the whiskey reflected more than just the pale light, it also managed to capture the faintest of outlines for the rags that I called clothes.

Patched together flannel and worn-down denim jeans, it was ok though, it went well with the house shoes that had not seen the outside world since two-thousand-thirteen, back when they still looked like they had any amount of life in them and probably didn't talk from the soles flapping. It was a combination where my three-day old beard in a slurry together with everything else, it just didn't grant the appearance that I wasn't living in my car at the time, it was all just a run of coincidence based on what I could grab immediately at the time that I got the telephone call. Coincidence was funny and fickle as a word, since it never really seemed to be on my side when I needed it the most, in fact I couldn't recall the last time that it ever made an appearance in my life as a saving grace. As the whiskey swished inside of my mouth from another sip tasting the blend of alcohol and oak, I had begun to wonder if she was going to show up at all considering the time of day. But then finally the door popped open almost as if the wind itself had grabbed it in a gust that wanted to find itself in the bar to sit amongst the patrons.

Coincidence was finally on my side as I turned around sluggishly to just notice her as she came in, getting up from my seat a little tipsy, it wasn't exactly the first set that I had since I walked into the bar. It was safe to say that it was in my best interest not to drive back to anywhere that I was going to be staying for the night, that much was for certain. Finally, I piped up in my confusion for the rushed meeting, in a voice grated by alcohol and tobacco, "sorry this is the only place I could think of, that would still be open at this hour, now would you mind giving me a somewhat straight story about what might be going on?" She seemed to be frazzled with her hair ruffled into a mess with it sticking out every which way, her beautiful azure dress didn't seem to quite match with the flow of her disheveled appearance. Then again, if looks were any kind of clue it was apparent that maybe this wasn't the first day of the week she had worn it, she rubbed her shoulder not even attempting to straighten her golden hair as her voice trickled out of her like a river bed that hadn't seen rain for a season or two, "sure... can we just get a booth?"

My left eyebrow arched at her demeanor, I just gestured with my hand as if to say lead the way, which I take it was understood since she started tiredly trudging off almost tensing the air around her as she went. Though I had been apt to follow her, as I watched her movements, I began to wonder how stressful this was going to be as I quickly trotted back and grabbed my drink before resuming to go to her.

"Alright Susan," rubbing my right eye in a rather elongated way like a TSA agent to a passenger at the airport patting them down in a so called anonymous search, "I took the day off already because you sounded like such a mess earlier, now I've known you and john for a long time, are you guys splitting up or something?"

Sipping on the whiskey that was keeping me going at this point, she seemed almost obtuse to a very basic question as if she didn't even hear me. Reluctant to make eye contact at first but a few moments later when she seemed suddenly ready to speak, I could see what I could only describe as complete and utter dismay, the kind of troubled look that finds you when you're looking into the abyss of loss.

"... Not exactly," as her voice started to catch a tremble amidst her syllables, "in fact i'm not even sure what's going on myself, but I think I've got to file a missing persons report." Her voice trailed off like a train that had just ran by the station with its whistle just continuing to fade in the distance as it chugged further away, the expression on her face seemed to spell out a nail that was being driven into her in the most unsubtle of ways, a nail called heartache. I grimaced a bit, I was never the one to be good with emotions, in fact I spent an awful lot of time trying to swallow them down in shots of relief served at liquor stores or bars. Then again, to whoever is reading this, I am sure you probably could have guessed that since I just woke up and started downing whiskey as a first response to being awake and alive yet again, that perhaps I had my own issues that needed solving. Trust me I get it, there are entirely better ways to deal with life and the disappointments that come with it, but at the end of the day, this isn't exactly my autobiography where I describe my rise and fall.

Shrugging my shoulders, arching that eyebrow even further, I realized my mouth became gawking at her and I probably didn't need to ask my next question, but I did anyway, "what do you mean you don't know? How do you not know if you need to file a missing persons report? He's your husband after all!" The alcohol had made me just a tad bit more insensitive and slightly louder as it usually did, an action that prompted a glare from the bartender. Louis always did like a quiet place, except if there were people doing poorly performed karaoke, on the return of my focus in her direction it became apparent that it had also prompted her to want to get up with tears streaming down her face. "I'm sorry Susan... please sit back down, tell me whatever you can, I mean has john been acting strange lately?"

She wouldn't look at me as I reached out taking her hand and I really did think it was me being halfcocked that had slighted her just enough to not want to speak anymore, but... I was wrong. Oh god was I wrong... she sniffled trying to keep the contents of her nose where they belonged while she looked down at her hands, pulling away from mine weakly, "strange is one way to put it, john hasn't been himself for quite some time."

As my utter bewilderment that had initially stunned me shifted into curiosity, I couldn't help myself but to belt out the most impressively awesome inquisitive question I could muster at the moment, "oh really?"

Her sigh could have blown a deck of cards off the table while she sat back down into her seat, which was only outdone in performative fashion by how it appeared that she was trying to stay awake, " I'm going to try and tell you the whole story James, but promise me you'll try not to call me crazy."

I couldn't help but laugh a little at her, "you woke me up at three in the morning for something you aren't even sure about, I think we are a little past the crazy marker, so just tell me whatever it is you've got to say, just try to keep in mind that I may have taken the day off but I do still have an A.A meeting where I have to pretend like I'm trying."

Smiling as I was, it still seemed my joke wasn't received nearly as well as I thought it would, she just kept looking down, appearing to be more and more lifeless as the seconds drove on in a long black Cadillac that had no intentions of ever looking back. She started on the subject anyway despite the expression resting on her face that seemed to showcase how much of a burden to her it was, "well last year, I think you know was our fifteenth year anniversary, we got my parents to watch the kids and we took a trip to Israel, we always wanted to see the place and all of the biblical landmarks." Her pause seemed rather cautionary for a brief moment as she chimed in again, "on the second to last day of the trip, on one of the many tours we were signed up for, we went through a desert that they practice the day of atonement, at one of the places we stopped there were some vendors along the road and our guide told us that we shouldn't buy anything from them because there have been known to be many con artists and thieves. Israel is apparently an expensive place to be, from what we were told."

"We couldn't really help it, or at least John couldn't, when we came across a withered old man who looked like he could barely afford the sandals that were loosely tied around his feet, he seemed honest to us. He said he was trying to sell replica pots of when Rome had its occupation, that he had always been a potter and after we went back and forth a few times, John convinced me. At least for the old mans' sake we should get something, John noticed a pot that had the symbol Saturn on it, and it seemed super authentic of age even though the man said he made them on his wheel. That was probably the first strange thing in a string of events, John just had to have that pot, even though the old man just kept refusing in the best English he could manage. Saying he wasn't sure if he could part with that pot as it had some kind of sentimental and apparently spiritual value to him, but he finally gave in and took John's money. Our tour guide wasn't very impressed with us in even the slightest, to say the least in terms of consequences from our little interaction with the old man who was selling pottery."

"When I walked away, I could still overhear them going back and forth between each other, I at the very least caught most of what was said in their prolonged conversation, the old man told him to be very careful with the pot, that if he just had to have it as a keepsake to remember a good time that he had. To make absolutely sure that the pot itself never had anything in it other than frankincense and myrrh, to never place a candle or something like that in it, It was a point that the old tired man spent quite a long period of time driving the fact home to John as important. Supposedly because the heat from the candle could destroy the quality of the pot, John asked why frankincense and myrrh, and the vendor struggled to understand at first. Then he laughed hoarsely and said it doesn't have to be that, put whatever you want in it just make sure never a candle. I really thought the old man was selling the candle a bit too well, like a superstition of sorts, but I let it go, just letting John have his pot as we got back on the bus and left. That wonderful place that took us to all of the sights, yet it also happened to be the place where we were berated by our tour guide for doing the one thing he advised us not to do because we could have been ripped off or led away to be killed in the desert."

Listening to her intently, this seemed to be an odd beginning to this whole thing as I swirled my whiskey in its glass, while scratching myself nonchalantly underneath my chin while she carried on.

"Well the rest of our trip was great, the next two days were wonderful, we then went to the airport to come back home and everything was seemingly good. We didn't even get hassled at customs about the pottery, when we finally got home, we ended up sleeping most of the day away, then we thought it would be nice if we used our last vacation day to take the kids out to eat. They were so excited about us coming back, their faces beamed with curiosity and their mouths had so many questions. They wanted to know everything, especially if we had gotten them any kinds of trinkets on our vacation, which would have been a yes if I hadn't received the voice mail earlier about the airport having lost track of our luggage, typical airport stuff you know? Well, when we came home, we tucked the kids into bed and a few days went by before the airport called saying they found our luggage around midafternoon. After John and I had finished up with work, we went to pick up the spoils of our trip showcasing all of the pictures and souvenirs to the kids that we'd collected on our journey. But when our oldest Sam who was only five tried to touch the pot, john got super possessive of it and said that he didn't want Sam to break the pot, he said I would hate to think that old man put all of his craftsmanship into this and we just broke it like it was nothing."

She seemed to freeze up at that last statement, a cold sadness hung in her eye like an icicle getting ready to fall, as I patiently waited for her to continue, a few minutes went by and then when I snapped my fingers, the cracking sound in the air made her jump a little bit.

"I'm sorry, I kind of spaced out a bit there, just that was one of the last times I remembered John being somewhat normal. Anyway, a couple months went by, and everything was ok I think until we got to Halloween. That's when things started to turn out down right odd, like how he reacted when Sam got curious that night and tried touching the pot. John put a candle stick in the pot, struck a match to light it before he killed the lights to tell the kids Sam and Rochelle scary stories after which he put them to bed. I wasn't exactly happy about super saturating them with sugar and nightmare fuel, but when he came back, he said he couldn't find the candle from earlier that he had placed inside of the pot to give the right ambiance for the kids. That night I felt him get out of bed and I thought he was just getting up to go to the bathroom, when he didn't come back, I thought I'd go see what was up, maybe the kids were out of bed sneaking Halloween candy or something. But no, he was down stairs on the couch hunched over and said that he had a splitting headache."

"I asked him, why don't you just take an aspirin or something? Come back to bed, it gets cold without you there and in the moonlight I just kind of saw him shrug, he muttered that's not all, I also had a very strange dream. I said why don't you tell me about it in the morning, but the next day he never did. For a long-time John kept saying he was having nightmares that he never would talk about, until I found him up one night at the pc and I was practically begging him to come to bed. In that moment I felt a shift in him as he started talking to me, when he looked me in the eye with his perpetually tired stare, his voice just dropped into the room like a surprise wrecking ball. You know Susan ... I have been shoved into a hole by force every night since Halloween and the only thing I could see in that darkness that was so thick was a candle, but I've noticed something, the candle keeps getting shorter every time I'm there." Finishing off my whiskey by now, I stopped her there, "so what you're saying is John was having some kind of psychotic experience coupled with night terrors? I mean if I'm following you correctly?"

She made eye contact with me however briefly, shrugging in a way that almost lined up with John in her story, "I'm not sure to be honest, I mean that's what I thought, but it's not like I'm a doctor or a therapist, I'm an accountant for a construction company."

I found myself positioning to say something sarcastic but I stopped myself, instead I said, "well if you think that John really has gone out of his mind, maybe you should put out a missing person for him, but I get it, this is all pretty odd, some rather strange behavior in a guy that you've decided to spend your life with." At this moment, that question about how stressful this was going to be finally reared its head with the ugly answer being yes, so I excused myself to go grab yet another whiskey from the bar, before returning to her wiping away the tears. Swishing back the mellowed oak over my tongue, i caught her off guard,

"I get it, this is all a lot, and I think you should probably go ahead with that missing persons report, because I'm beginning to suspect that may be the only way to get the answers you're really looking for."

She cleared her throat, slapping back my suggestion in a way that was reminiscent of a woman that had just caught her man cheating, sternly stating, "let me finish."

I took the loss of trying to persuade her to do the sensible thing in that moment as I tossed up my hands and said, "ok," rather obediently, not putting up that much of a fight against her, especially with her already being so distraught.

She then resumed her story with that meek tiny voice, which I really had to focus on, "anyway I recommended that John go to get therapy and maybe some meds, because he was starting to scare both me and the kids. John didn't put up a fight against it. He would end up getting put on a thousand milligrams of tranquilizers, only, he would never go to sleep and said that if he did, he knew exactly what was going to happen. John began missing work, eventually never leaving the house. I really thought it was some kind of social anxiety brought on by the insomnia that he had yet to be cured of. It seemed nothing was helping, and the more and more John went to therapy, which soon became a daily thing, the more and more the doctors thought he was schizophrenic. They said that John was complaining of voices and shadows moving about, that the meds should help him. But they were wrong on so many levels, call it a case of educated idiots trying to diagnose something, as he only kept sliding down that slippery slope, he went from being the John we know to looking like someone who was being mummified alive."

She appeared to be choking back tears for yet another time, to be honest I had lost count at this point in the story of how many times she was crying or trying not to, twiddling her thumbs almost nervously looking down again.

Like shame had her in a vise grip, it was almost as if she felt somewhere she could have done more, at least if how she was acting had any kind of a story to tell on its own.

I leaned over trying to inflect the needed soft caring into the tones of my voice and said, " you know, if this is too hard you don't have to say it."

She offered something back to me, sniffles that remained reminiscent of an allergy season that no one else was suffering from and only muttered, "no it's ok, I think you should know, since we haven't spoken in so long." Wiping her nose with a bar napkin that tinged her skin a rose color, " I had such high hopes that John would just get better, but he never did, he just kept falling into the abyss while we reached out for him. Then just a few days ago when I came home, he was just placidly on the couch staring blankly, alone in the dark, holding that stupid pot, when I walked up to him, he turned away from me with a melancholic sigh that felt like it was going to rattle the house apart. When I tried to turn on the lights, his voice was calm like a psychopath's lullaby, serendipitously he spat out that he killed the breaker, the lights hurt my eyes. I tried to ask John if he was ok but the hissing of a shh was what prattled out, as if things couldn't have gotten stranger, he started rambling incoherently in a mess of words tangled together. But what finally gripped me and grabbed my breath, was when I felt his eyes cutting through the shadows directly into my eyes saying why don't you come sit down with me my dear, it gets so lonely in the dark. I mean after being in there for so long you have a tendency to forget that there is light, in fact, you even start to hate it."

"Walking up closer, I noticed there was something wrong with his eye's, although I couldn't really place it in the darkness of the evening mixed with a house that had no lights, I began backing away as I said ok John you're starting to weird me out a little too much. His scurrying feet swept up to an arm's length away where that hiss of a shush greeted me again that tumbled into a cackle, his eyes shined in the dark as his unclouded voice somehow echoed in my head, Susan, Susan, Susan, John isn't home right now, please leave a message at the tone of the beep. Ha-ha just kidding, John is in here kicking around, you know at first that candle was just an everyday thing, and now he clings onto it for dear life, like the flame won't eventually splutter and fade. He began Sporadically laughing and moving, as I started to edge around where he had shuffled to in the darkness, starting towards the stairs to go up so I could check the kids, when he sent lightning through me with his words, oh those kids, Susan they aren't here, no worries they aren't here to see their precious father go off his metaphorical rocker, although I think we both know one of them, the oldest isn't really his, now are they? Aww, don't beat yourself up too bad Susan, God knows you humans are always such a treat to watch, in fact I even came down to teach you guys once upon a time, only to get shoved into a dirty little hole and covered up with rocks and earth. It's alright, though I've done my time and pretty soon John will do his, after all, the old man did warn you about not putting a candle in the vessel didn't he?"

"Trembling as the fear coursed through me like a raging river at this point, I backed out, towards the front door, and I could still hear John's voice going on in a callous gravel tone. Did you really think you could put a light in the darkness and not expect to have something come and pick it up?! His maniacal laugh stretched like rubber as he picked up his words again, don't run away Susan! Don't do that, lord knows you believe in God almighty, but this right here, this right here! You'll try to rationalize it as some mental illness, I mean what else could it be. Not to worry Susan, me and John will be waiting, as a distant whisper came from behind dripping into my ear methodically saying, after all, it gets lonely in the dark. The lights snapped back on, like it was the end of a magic trick, all the appliances were beeping as they turned back on, and John was gone, so I'm not sure.... But I think I need to do a missing persons report."

Sitting there with an empty glass as the bartender started to holler out about it being closing time, silence brewed itself into the mix shortly after, until I broke it with, "That is certainly quite the story you've uhm got there Susan. Sounds like quite the story, uh yeah, I guess a missing persons report is the way to go," as we got up and left the bar making our way out into the shadow painted streets of the city. She traipsed in front of me not yet responding, "so if it was so obvious the way you needed to go about this whole thing, why did you come here to get confirmation or whatever from me?"

An auditory confusion of which she didn't turn around to greet at first, then suddenly she stopped which almost made me rear end her as she stayed pointed away from me, slowly saying in a low tone, "to be honest, I don't think they are going to find john ever. I just didn't want to be alone," her voice faded off like a whisper in the dark, she'd been doing that for practically the whole night. It was then she turned and beamed at me with radiant desert golden eye, "after all it gets lonely in the dark, and I need somebody to hold me, you'll come by and hold me won't you?"

I wasn't very sure how to react at first, as it's not like she was touching me, but I felt a firm icy grip on me, I quelled any fear and surprise or even excitement, because the reason we weren't together is because John and her were together. I remarked as confused as a schoolboy who was talking to a girl for the first time, "umm sure why not, right, I'll follow you in my car," as the nervous laugh crept out of my mouth.

Her frozen smile hung in my mind as she walked off to her car, she got in and proceeded to take off in the direction of their house. I shuffled off to mine like molasses in the winter breeze and I didn't hold up my end of our conversation at all, in fact maybe I should reiterate exactly why I had the feeling of surprise and carnal fear. I've known Susan almost my entire life, she has been one of the sweetest and kindest individuals I have ever known and once upon a time we even were going to get married, we knew everything about one another at a certain time in our lives, and one thing I can tell you is her eyes were always blue. I'm not terribly certain what occurred to me, but despite relentless phone calls and text messages I was not and am not, I repeat am not going over there to keep anyone company in the dark as it was put. I put a little time and research into everything to try and make sense of it all, as a matter of fact, I've even missed a few days of work doing research, I haven't got much sleep.

But going off what she had to say, maybe john hadn't lost his mind after all, maybe he was being tormented by a demon that was once a watcher, for those of you who don't know a watcher was an angel. In fact, it was a very specific class of angel, that was meticulously tasked with keeping tabs on mankind, but they all failed in their duties by doing great sins as they were called in the book of Enoch. Teaching them magics to usurp the natural order of the world, taking mortal women for their beauty to procreate and have children that towered above the rest of the living globe. It was a time of debauchery so fierce that the creator of the world sought to wipe it all away to alleviate the plight of darkness that swept across the lands like a flood seeking out any light it could to possibly feed on. Enoch was sent to tell them of their great crimes and judgment that was coming to rain down on them quite literally, letting water stack up like bricks to a mausoleum for them to be laid to rest in for the upcoming eons that the earth would spin.

Their leader was Azazel, who if you look hard enough around for, you can see that the Romans personified him as Saturn, he's had plenty of other names as well, I'm not entirely sure how or why he escaped his earthly prison. The one that he was pushed into with jagged rocks, and covered up with dirt, if I had to say for certain it had something to do with the candle. The fact that light was cast out, attracting him just like a moth into an unwavering shrinking flame, just like John was alluding to before he disappeared, and as of now it seems as though he is on the search for a new vessel having been released. He was probably in Susan before he came into contact with me to spread fear, mixing in night terrors so surreal that it's like you're in your own horror movie and it makes perfect sense after all the watchers as they were called, are ones who never sleep. These intense vivid nightmares, if this is what john was going through, I can totally understand why he wouldn't want to talk about any of it.

Sometimes I think if I look closely enough, I can see the darkness creeping around the corner just a little bit out of the reach of my sight, wrapping up against the wall with tendrils of a monster that hasn't been documented yet. The nightmares are so unrelenting, you're standing before an open maw of a pit and then soon you're standing in the pit with those radiating yellow eyes, watching you as you make your way to the waning candle. It never blinks, it never looks away, and you can feel the chill from a smile you can never attempt to even try to see as you pick up the candle and try to walk closer. He is forever moving away, yet somehow always approaching like a lion in the savannah stalking down its prey with magic foot work, that you'd need a detailed explanation from a master of illusion about, and then, you still probably wouldn't understand. When you're awake he's there scratching at the back of your mind like a scab that refuses to heal, just throbbing with the need for relief, but you can't take a nap or else you're bearing down on the scab, making it worse.

Though I suppose it's not as bad as it could be, with all the things going on in the world beyond the realms of our control, it can be comforting to know that something is constant and unwavering. Like the soft hum of a distant song that you've forgotten, nibbling at corners of your ears, a symphonic melody that tones out the rest of the world in a timeless fashion. Washing you in comfort like a mid-summer breeze snaking its way through the grass where you can be relaxed in a lawn chair underneath the shade of a tree that you never had to plant, massaging across your skin in a way that reminds you of childhood. I know this change is so sudden from what I was writing before, it just never occurred to me while I was lost in the motions that maybe this was all misunderstood, maybe John and Susan were right all along to give in the way they did. So take a minute and hear me out, sit a spell and trace the words with your eyes, follow along now because now I am a believer.

If you're still reading this my friend, don't be afraid of him, I mean after all he loves me, you, and everybody else on earth, I mean he stepped down so he could teach us all, in the ways we were ignorant. Taught us how to work with metals for technological advancement, he tutored women on how to be as beautiful as they are today and even showed us the best stones. He was our Prometheus showing up to show us how to be modern and how to advance with the secrets of the heavens, laying everything bare before our eyes and lifting the curtain on our ignorance. He even knew the steep price he might have to pay, but he gladly did it anyway for the sake of humankind, so that we could know that we were capable of anything. Set aside your reservations, what are you waiting for, light a candle and say hello, let him in, after all he's spent a long time away from us, and it gets lonely in the dark.

Avarice inc.

The alarm clock rang out through the room with the sudden burst of Frank Sinatra I don't dance from the oldies station it had been set to from the day it was brought to the then-new home on that cold December day Daniel had moved into his apartment. Music which was almost entirely shrouded by the hammering rain coming down on that mid-April morning, Daniel had barely even heard it, even after it changed songs for nearly fifteen minutes. By the time, his bleary hazel wood eyes opened, it had made its way to the Chordettes hit song lollipop, another of his personal favorites.

Ruffled red hair from the tossing and turning at night, anticipating today with all his excitement, he reluctantly despite his antsy nature, fell asleep. All due to last night's notification on his Samsung Galaxy phone which said that his shipment of books would be arriving today, fortunately, it coincidentally happened to be one of his days off. A decent turn of events since package theft was a little bit of a problem at his apartment complex, after all was said and done he pulled a decent amount of money at a locally owned restaurant as a cook. However, it would never be enough to cover all of his packages that had gone missing, to take that grand old second attempt of getting something he had paid for.

A pale white hand slathered with freckles slapped down on the off button of the alarm clock, the average yet gangly ginger featured man in his yogi bear pajamas arose from his full-sized bed decorated with a custom Deadpool comforter and matching pillowcase set. Passing by the modern styled bookshelves that lined his left wall, semi filled with books, more so lined with a particular series of comic books, mainly featuring the same peculiar character from his bed set that he had spent what seemed like an eternity collecting. Passing through the doorway with his hand accidentally brushing on the desk that also had his desktop computer he had custom-built; it was but a short distance to the bathroom in this one-bedroom apartment that he had finally made feel like home, despite the setbacks that had popped up along the way. Stopping in the view of the mirror to admire himself, the urge to stroke his ego was far too great, with Daniel speaking to his reflection in his oddly placed baritone voice, "you're getting older, but damn you still look good buddy," the tension down below suddenly reminded him that his bladder was the real reason that he had gotten up out of bed in the first place.

The time itself could not actually be told by the sun due to the weather going on outside, though it was his routine to get up at nine A.M religiously whether he was working or not, something he had learned in his early twenties. That way he could always have the time to get ready, he found it to be an insurance against the things that could happen, ever since Rebecca had left him and he went through that great depression, his routine he had set up years earlier was the anchor that kept that storm of his life from blowing him away. Finishing up with his bladder in an aim less than perfect, he had to bend down to wipe the seat. At that moment however, his lower colon suddenly didn't have a taste for Chinese food, the wonderfully bright idea he decided to have for his dinner last night. Slightly agitated he groaned, "I swear, why can't I ever just go to the bathroom all at once?" Taking a seat, he heard a knock at the door and simultaneously heard his phone on his nightstand go off with Captain America, "Avengers unite!" Which was followed up immediately by Daniel exclaiming, "god damn it!" It was a myriad of noise that came swirling into his ears at the most inopportune time, Murphy and his law always had a fine way of hitting him in the jewels, and it was always at the worst possible moment for it to occur.

Hurrying up with his surprise from last night's dinner, he washed his hands with the bar of dial soap sitting on the sink, drying his hands hastily with the brown hand towel hanging on the rack above the toilet, this was the first time in a while since he had been this excited. Turning both deadbolts and the lock on the handle of the door, he opened it up to the concrete pathway leading to his door in Salem New Hampshire, without a UPS man anywhere in sight. Looking down, his face lit up with joy as he bent down and picked up the box marked from Amazon.com and then a slight look of confusion as he suddenly noticed a much smaller box on the side of the door frame. The box was marked for his address in a plain brown cardboard box with a shipping label clearly marked for him and his address as he picked it up and inspected it somewhat thoroughly.

Taking both packages inside to his unremarkable kitchen table set and setting them down, he decided to go into the kitchen in the small one-bedroom grabbing a steak knife from a kitchen drawer that needed to find a sharpener. Diving into the amazon box first since that was what he was eagerly awaiting, he finally finished his collection of Victor Hugo by adding toilers at sea to the one of his many bookshelves in his bedroom. A first edition of the American Gods collection by Neil Gaiman and two

Deadpool mint condition comic books he had been searching forever for, Deadpool kills the marvel universe and Deadpool issue number one.

Though if Daniel was honest with himself those comic book originals were about to go down in major value since they were about to be removed from their packaging and read about his favorite anti-hero that had always fascinated him since he was a teenager. However, curiosity was now eating Daniel even to the point where he openly asked himself the question out loud, "I wonder what is in the other box? I really don't remember ordering anything else that would have been shipped differently." Daniel made his way back to the kitchen to scan the box over once again, this time he noticed the name of the shipper as Avarice.inc as he remarked to himself somewhat bewildered, "sounds like some kind of investment company." Before using that same dull kitchen steak knife to open the box, to which he found another book, something that should have filled him with glee, instead it was replaced with morbid curiosity. Bound in black leather with gold brimming the edges of a book an inch and a quarter thick, it almost seemed like it could be some weird knock off of some religious text, maybe something belonging to a cult. He opened it up, finding the title page which read Avarice.inc a book for greed, followed by underneath it in italicized text the only book you will ever need, flipping beyond to the next page in his skeptical gaze. There appeared to be a poem of sorts, which read:

A friend in need is a friend indeed,
however, before you cultivate the seed.
Remember there is a price for greed,
From lucre to women or a stairway to heaven.

Greed is any strong want or need,
Which can bring despair the size of a sea.
Take great care of this book you received,
From fame to any setting be careful where you are treading.

After finishing the brief piece of poetry which to be honest, he was not even sure if he felt was all that great to begin with, he flipped to the next page finding it blank all the way to the end where he found the stamp of Avarice.inc followed by a one eight hundred number. "Alright well that was a creepy little piece of poetry," he remarked to himself as Daniel made his way to where his phone was set down on the nightstand in his room. "But that's alright, I am sure this was probably sent here by mistake, so I guess we will give them a call and get this all sorted out." Picking up the phone and walking casually back to the book he punched in the number after which he realized was quite literally 1-800-Avarice. A coincidence that brought a brief chuckle before mashing the call button while he sarcastically thought *oh how cute a custom telephone line.*

The phone rang twice with a quite pleasant and rather cute British female voice picking up on the other end, "hello, this is Veronica, thanks for calling Avarice.inc where a friend in need is a friend indeed and how is our friend Daniel Schmidt today?" Her voice echoed through the speaker holes of the phone reverberating off of his ear drum in such a manner that it was a stunning force, an auditory taser to his brain.

Daniel froze in place for a moment, stunned by a high voltage shock of unease. Wondering how in the world they could have known his name and then his brain finally clicked as he remembered the world of caller ID, which let him push out a relieved sigh followed by his answer, "yes veronica, I am actually calling about the book." With his New England accent growing thicker— as it always did around women, especially ones with candy toned voices, "I think I might have got this book by mistake."

Expecting a pause in the flow of conversation he was drastically surprised as Veronica responded instantly in her cheerful tones, "there are no mistakes at Avarice.inc sir, a friend saw that you were in need and asked that we send you our limited-edition book only for the choicest of audiences."

Growing a puzzled look on his face, Daniel responded in the most intellectual question he could muster, "uh . . . say what now?" Before correcting himself, "I guess what I mean to say is, I don't think I understand the book, there is a little poem in the front and then nothing, is it like a journal, some weird pseudo intellectual self-help book where you actually help yourself?" It almost felt like it should have been an easy question to answer in the grand scheme of things, but his brain seemed to be struggling like an overweight truck trying to roll up a hill.

Veronica's tone on the other end of the line never shifted from the ever-cheerful voice. She responded, "most of our friends find it to be the best self help book they've ever used; in fact, they even describe it as the most helpful book they have ever had." Though clear and concise with her words that softly cut through the question he had posed to her, it did nothing to erase the confusion growing on Daniels face–or for that matter even the heightening confusion in his mind. To which Daniel was about to shoot off another question to maybe gain himself some more clarity on the nature of the book, but Veronica cut him off with the answer, "just write what you want in the book and then you can have it, friend, it's that easy."

Daniel's brain finally seemed to click into place on the subject like two jigsaw pieces that finally got lined up. "Oh! So you mean like the law of attraction or that kind of thing? You know I've actually heard a lot about this, so it is like a self-help book," with his words rolling off of a sarcastic tongue.

Veronica with her permanent marker demeanor in its notes of cheerfulness, sweetly replied to him, "If that's how you'd like to see it, yes, it is like the law of attraction except if you write it in *this* book, you'll have much better results."

This kind of an answer gave Daniel the feeling that he was just going to go in circles with the woman, with that thought in mind he decided it was almost time to end the call, but not before the question sprang to mind. Who could have possibly thought he needed this pseudo intellectual garbage?

Veronica however, despite her witty english accent was quick on the draw like an old western gunslinger. She responded, "We don't give out friends' details sir. We appreciate you not asking, as part of our confidentiality and *yours*. Is there anything else I can help you with today, sir?"

Daniel was taken back a bit in surprise as though she had just read his mind to know what he was going to ask, logic however, came around the bend into the conversation where he figured it must have been a common question and brushed it off as just an interesting coincidence. There was not much else he could muster, in terms of trying to figure out this book, and so Daniel said, "no thank you I guess, that will be all."

Veronica replied absolutely chipper, "Anytime Mr. Schmidt, if you ever need help with the book, feel free to give us a call back at Avarice.inc. Where a friend in need is a friend indeed."

As the line went dead. Daniel thought, *well her customer service was great right up until the end there*. Taking another look in the book, he put it back on his kitchen table to keep the salt and pepper shaker company. "Alrighty then. *That* answered a lot of questions." Daniel rolled his eyes in dismay, being slightly weirded out by the entire conversation that had just occurred. Despite the oddity he found shortly thereafter his attention had shifted back toward ruining comic books that would ultimately be better off staying in the packaging. Hours passed as Daniel toyed away the day with all the new novelties in literature, but eventually the amusement faded, as it became overcast by his stomach growling as if it were the beginnings of a thunderstorm. Daniel put away his new sources of amusement and proceeded into the kitchen, since he had never truly learned to cook or portion for just one person, Hawaiian pork over rice that could have fed an army came out instead. Sitting down to eat at the table, right in his view was a steaming plate of sweet and savory sat down in the company of a book that in all of his wits paired off with his questions, he had absolutely zero answers for.

Daniel sat there as he slowly ate his food, feeling suddenly a vibe as if though the book itself was oddly staring out at him burning a hole into him with phantasmal eyes. Which was a very uncomfortable and beguiling feeling that made his skin prickle. Mid chew, Daniel said aloud "you know I suppose, I could use this thing as like a notebook or a journal." After that jest, a statement of purpose for the book, the feeling seemed to slowly sink back into the depths, almost as if the book had been satiated by the notion that Daniel would find a use for it. After dinner he put the leftovers away into his apartment's supplied white fridge. Daniel immediately after began searching for a pen to at least be able to clip to the book, though it should have been easy. It quickly became an annoyance that culminated in him pairing the book with a pen he knew only worked when it felt like it. Grumbling while he shuffled off to bed for the night. He needed sleep. Tomorrow's shift lay just a few hours away, almost within his fingers' reach, shutting off the lights as he meandered toward his bedroom . Though probability with its percentages had spurned him in the search for a pen, fate had been kind. He'd spent the day in his pajamas, so no need to change. After he fell into bed, he set his alarm, plugged his phone in, and drifted to sleep.

The night passed by too quickly with the hours draining in a cyclone toward the drain, Daniel found himself having one of the sweetest of dreams he could have, a world where he owned a comic bookstore of his very own. The alarm clock had its own predesignated plan as it blared the oldies station, and with a cruel electronic rudeness yanked him from his dreams. Today was a change back to his common routine since Daniel had to go to work, he laid there momentarily just as bleary-eyed as so many days before. Eventually he found his footing and headed for a shower and shave. Reemerging back out of the steam from the shower, he got dressed in his work uniform– a white button-up shirt, black slacks that he methodically put the crease into, with a belt. A careful examination in the mirror to make sure everything was in place, he was about to leave, revealed that he had missed just a couple of whiskers during his shave. He always had an eye for detail–though It was times like this that made him wish that he could turn a blind eye to the little things. With a smile, he tried injecting some positivity toward the start of the day as he winked at himself in the mirror and said,

"Let's try to make this a good day."

Rest assured of his looks; he found his keys in their usual spot on top of the fridge in the kitchen, even though sometimes they got pushed a little farther back and he could swear up and down that someone stole them. He walked out of the hallway, popping out the front door after the ritual unlocking process. A swift turn-around followed for the ritualistic relock. When suddenly he realized that he had forgotten his phone on the nightstand, an absent-minded move that he would chastise himself about at some point, despite the rituals and routines it seemed as though sometimes the most basic things for his daily life were forgotten the most. Turning around with the sigh that left his lips, he turned all three locks and briskly walked back in, when he nearly tripped in surprise by the book he knew he left on the table, So how did it end up in the hallway? Firmly clutched in his right hand, he tucked it under his arm despite the abnormality of it, simply because he did not feel as though he really had the time to spare, it was the risk of showing up late to work that rattled in his brain, which in his eyes was as deadly as any sin mankind had ever thought up.

In a rush to retrieve his phone off the bedroom nightstand, he haphazardly took it off the charger, shoving it in his right pants pocket before heading back out, this time making it to his blue 2013 Toyota Supra. Unlocking the car, he practically jumped in while he tossed the book into the passenger seat as he started it up and drove eight minutes down the road with that single right turn into the restaurant parking lot on policy street, just past the theme park. McCallister's was always busy because of that theme park, the fact was that people simply didn't want to pay for the overpriced fair themed food. Though he never thought of it very often, let alone while he looked for a place to park, realistically it was probably the reason why they could actually pay the cooks there a living wage. After a few moments of his wandering thoughts, he eyed a parking spot that he gladly took, finally with the car in park he looked at the clock on the radio of his car. Realizing that after that fiasco of forgetting his phone, he was twenty minutes early still, shadowed behind the light of his perfectionist ways, that twenty minutes on the clock was still considered five minutes too late to him.

Glancing over to that black and gold book in his passenger seat with a sneer, now officially where he needed to be for the moment, " you just behave yourself, you creepy little book."

Daniel hurriedly got out of his car, hearing the alarm sound from the remote button of his keys as he headed inside to deal with the same aggravating coworkers he never felt really pulled their weight around the place. His shift went for the most part alright, though Ron, had rubbed his nerves raw for repeatedly not making food to recipe and playing the kinds of games that would be reminiscent of school children with his other co-worker Mark. It was things like this as to why he always had to not only just focus on the dish he was preparing, but also theirs as well multiple times throughout the day. The waiting staff was less than well manned as well, they usually needed the occasional cook to go out and serve the food, Daniel always seemed to draw the short lot on that duty. Jonathan tried to hammer it home that it was only because he could "*rely*" on Daniel to multi-task. The extra effort had led to multiple pay raises, so Daniel did tolerate it better than if he was getting nothing. It was in no way extreme or equal to the amount of extra workload placed on him by Jonathan's overall poor management skills, the same restaurant that his father owned, the same place that was always in disarray but who keeps track of that sort of thing, certainly not a perfectionist who thought out everything they did one hundred times or more.

Finally catching a break after all the rushes they had that day, Daniel slipped outside to his car feeling like he was going to explode from all the extra nonsense from his co-workers Ron and Mark. Jonathan had even told him to, "take an extra ten if he needed it."

It had become obvious even to Jonathan how the chaos had gotten to Daniel over the course of the day that steam could almost be seen exiting his ears. Finally in the solitude of his car, Creedence Clearwater Revival's "Have You Ever Seen the Rain?" poured out of the speakers of his car. Daniel pawed at the book in his passenger seat before getting a firm grip, still nursing his anger like a bitter child. The feeling swept over him in a wave, that if he wrote it down, it would be out of his system, and just maybe he could go back to work. Fifteen minutes into his break, he opened up that tar black leather-bound book to the first blank page and jotted the words down.

I swear to God I wish that I worked with people that actually knew what in the hell they were doing and were competent at their jobs.

He attempted to squiggle out various other complaints, the page only seemed interested in recording the part about people being competent at their jobs. Which only poured salt in the wound of the day that had already been thus far. Daniel wrestled with the pen in order for it to write as he exclaimed with the meager froth of vitriol inside of his car, "Great! Now the goddamn pen works as hard as my co-workers."

Daniels' break had drawn to a close. He took a few deep breaths and exhaled letting the anger just vent away, before making his way back inside the restaurant. His keen eyes that held a magnetism for details didn't notice it at first. The usual people bused tables—with greater attention to detail, the pep in their step couldn't be denied, the words, "abnormal efficiency," leaked out of his mouth under his breath. When he passed by Jonathan's office on the way to the kitchen, he couldn't help but notice something different. Jonathan seemed to have vanished. He had been replaced by Robert, his seventy-year-old father who had somehow managed to retain all his hair, dressed in a black casual business attire that pressed up against his white skin. It was a sight that stopped Daniel in his tracks, his eyebrow arched while his hand lightly knocked on the side of the door. Uncertain of this abnormal visit his voice cracked out, "Uh, hello, sir… it's a pleasure to see you, where did Jonathan take off to?"

The soft-spoken elderly man also seemed befuddled, it was as if Daniel's question had landed on the ears of someone from a parallel universe, which only seemed elaborated by the pause. He replied, "well it's good to see you too my little Tom Brady, but what are you talking about?"

Daniels' confusion began to rise like the old faithful geyser in Yellowstone Park. His voice crept out like a child trying to keep the secret of them being awake at midnight on a school night. "You know, Jonathan, your son. Where is he? I thought he was still here."

An overall question that from Daniel's perspective was entirely innocent and shouldn't have been too hard to have an answer thrown back at him. Even if Robert was Seventy and couldn't necessarily throw a ball literally due to arthritis, he knew that he still possessed the mental faculties to be witty and downright quick with his words if need be.

His response grabbed Daniel by surprise, Robert's words were a home invader at midnight with the shock they were going to induce. Robert, visibly concerned for Daniel, let the words cautiously out of his mouth, "Jonathan god though I love him has had a drug problem all of his life and is in prison, he's never stepped foot inside this office."

For a moment Daniel wasn't quite sure that he had heard Robert correctly, there was a certain buzzing in his ears like after a bomb got detonated without any kind of plug for protection. Through his blatant confusion, his words tripped almost over themselves with his question, "Could you repeat that?"

It was as if Atlas had finally shrugged the cosmos off of his shoulders, allowing it to hit the earth with tumultuous quakes rippling through the very fiber of Daniel's brain. Robert, with his face twisting into an unamused expression to be answering this sort of thing, explained Jonathan's newly unveiled sordid past, tales of his dealings that ended him up in prison. The FBI raid that came down faster than Thor's hammer, breaking up a drug ring he had been running out of a trap house in Worcester, Massachusetts. How Robert had to testify against his own son alongside so many others that knew him from finger cuttings to other mutilations that expressed a corrupt pull for money and power, which ultimately led to a twenty-five-year minimum prison sentence. Those quakes from the sudden shift that had ripped through Daniel were pressing in their aftershocks, making everything just quake with an anxiety that he didn't even know he was capable of.

Daniel shifted into a pale shade comparable to someone being laid in the grave as though he'd been living in a dream and had just snapped back to reality.

Robert asked, "Are you feeling alright? I mean you were there for those hard times— for me *and* the misses."

Daniel began to reel as his stomach churned with a sickness he'd never felt he'd known before. What in the world was going on? One moment he had been at the place he'd been working at for the last eight years where he had his own rise and fall, and the next, he found himself in a parallel universe that seemed equipped with its own startling duality. Daniel muttered, "yeah... yeah I think I am ok, but I think I really need to sit down, though."

Robert let out a hushed chuckle, "Might need to get some sugar in your system, working as hard as you do. I'm surprised you find the time to eat. But go ahead sit down, this is your office after all. I just thought I'd stop in and see how business was going."

Daniel's head spun like a top as if the devil himself had full possession of him in his grasp. A marionette dangling from the fingertips of a cruel puppeteer that made him stumble in the whirlwind of a world he had suddenly lost his footing in.

Robert, noticing Daniel on his way to the ground as though he'd been uppercut by a poltergeist chimed in, "Listen I think maybe you've been hitting the books and this place a little too hard. Maybe let this old man close her down tonight huh? Why don't you go home and get some rest?"

Daniel, though some part of his mind still wanted to try and finish his shift after getting knocked off of his horse, he just couldn't argue with this suggestion. This was way too much to process now and he couldn't keep going if these panic attacks were going to keep beating him down like a UFC fighter trying to take home a belt. At a loss for words, Daniel simply nodded his head, and then after a moment, his voice as if he hadn't had a drink of water in three or four days, said, " I think I'll do that, thank you sir." Daniel's feet made his way out to his car like a drunken sailor in a port town, with the fading words of Robert behind him telling him to, "rest up." Once safely back in his car, he glanced over at the book and then his gaze settled off blankly on the wheel. "What... just happened?" This was the first and only time he had ever truly felt lost, he wrote something down and suddenly the world was different as if everything had been shifted around for *his* benefit. Over the next 30 minutes Daniel continued to ruminate on the events that had just occurred. He snatched up the book, switched on the dome light, and flipped open the book to the first page. With the remnants of anxiety adding a shifting sand quality to his voice, he read the poem again aloud.

> A friend in need is a friend indeed,
> however, before you cultivate the seed.
> Remember there is a price for greed,
> From lucre to women or a stairway to heaven.
>
> Greed is any strong want or need,
> Which can bring despair the size of a sea.
> Take great care of this book you received,
> From fame to any setting be careful where you are treading.

As his eyes steadily grew wider with the reverberation of the words from the poem. Softly the words slipped through his lips toward the book in his hands with the question, "what in the hell are you?" In a matter of mere moments Daniel's life had been rearranged as if it had always been that way. The unshakeable feeling gripped him, the book seemed to radiate almost as if it was smiling, staring him down with an enticingly evil stare. It was almost like it could speak, whispering in the white noise of the evening, begging for pages to be filled out, slathering on sweet silent soliloquies in an attempt to see what he would really do. But at what kind of cost? Daniel most definitely received what he desired, but in the midst of that desire was someone who was caught in the crossfire of the desire he wrote down. The thought had even crossed his mind that perhaps this was a nervous breakdown of sorts, that this was all some form of psychosis. The nail in his chest was the turn of events for Jonathan, a man that had been nothing but good to him despite his over reliance on daniel. It was puck sliding down the ice for a cold win, where life had slid seemingly unbidden in Daniels favor.

His hands rattled like a beat down car going down the highway as he stuck the key into the ignition. The slow drive home took fifteen minutes longer than needed and was bathed in the sound of a silent radio that lit up the car flashing its songs as they played. He found his usual parking spot and grabbed the book that at this moment he didn't want anywhere near him. As he went through the motions of getting out of the car and starting his walk, he didn't even bother setting the car alarm. He slowly drifted through the parking lot as a sullen man, the night air and the wandering mind found his sulking interrupted by his apartment door, where he attempted to slide in his key only to find it no longer worked. In fact, not a single one of his keys worked in the slightest. Another turn of events in the evening that made Daniel let out a groan that felt more like he was exhaling lead vapor into the mid-April night, it was just another scene in a new play he had not rehearsed for. Despite the exhale, his chest felt as though it was being binded under an intense gravity, as if the groans and sighs themselves made his breathing ponderous while his mind continuously shifted back to Jonathan and his newly found woes.

His thoughts found themselves interrupted when he heard someone on the inside of the apartment that used to be his exclaim some indistinguishable words, more than likely from the sound of someone trying to get inside the place. At that moment, Daniel wasn't entirely sure his confusion could grow anymore, not to mention the other emotions swelling up inside of him like a bee sting that still had the stinger in it. He laid a knock against the door. A moment later the door locks slid open along with the door.

A young African American man yelled, "Fucking A, man! It's ten o'clock at night, are you looking to get shot?"

Daniel heaved with a heavy-laden sigh. Clearly this was no longer his apartment, another par for the course he seemed to be on. He Rubbed his forehead, visibly shaken from the night's events as tears began to well in the corner of his eyes.

The demeanor of the man at the door calmed after getting a good look at Daniel. He said, "I'm sorry my guy, it looks like you've had a rough night already. What's got you at my door at this time of night?"

Daniel was flabbergasted, drawing so many blanks in a row without even an iota of an explanation to be had, so he blurted, "You wouldn't happen to know which door is mine, would you?"

The young man had now officially drunk out of the same cup that held Daniel's confusion. He asked," Are you wicked twisted my guy? You live upstairs where the two bedrooms are. I see you here all the time. Shit, we talk at the mailbox sometimes, your old lady has probably been waiting on you, I think you're two-fourteen."

His response at that point didn't faze Daniel, given the day was filled with blurred lines of reality that no longer matched what he'd known. Who said, "thanks for the help man, it's uhm... been a long day"

The young man furrowed his brow on widening eyes of concern, "Sounds like it, go get some sleep my guy."

Daniel was turning on his heels, heading back up another flight of stairs to two-fourteen. His keys fit into the door like a hand into a glove. The door opening wafted the greeting of a familiar scent, It was jasmine and cedar wood, a scent that to him could only belong to one person. The scent was followed by her voice that came from off around the right corner of the hallway. Rebecca's voice. a voice he knew all too well, with its fresh butter caramel warm tone.

"Hey! I didn't expect you back so soon, Mr. Schmidt," she said playfully—just as Daniel had remembered so fondly in all the times he reminisced.

The same scenes played out all the way back in Daniel's memories that often found him while he was falling through the depths of the most pleasant of dreams. Despite all of the pleasantries of this newfound universe in which Daniel found himself, he couldn't deny the guilt eating at the back of his brain, it was a parasite draining the joy out this moment. She approached him from around the corner out of the hallway. Her long flowing night black hair and sultry green eyes that always seemed to make his heart melt. Her full lips pursed as she greeted him with a kiss that made his heart practically leap from his chest.

"How was your day at work?" she asked.

"Let's just say it was a little confusing," Daniel replied, no longer shaken by his nerves. He found himself suddenly embracing the madness, this crazy new world. The entire world flipping, showing the inverse picture of the life he had grown to accept seemed to fade away into a dull pain. To be honest with his most true self, this was an embrace he had missed the most, it was the main reason he had stayed single. She had, after all, left him, where he soaked in the waters of his own misery with the claims that he would never amount to much echoing on their tides.

A momentary lapse that made his head find its center, despite the seemingly endless boon that had found him from the ether. A line written in a dark foreboding book that exuded a heavy aura, a far cry from the essence of who he was, prevented him from savoring the present moment. His head gravitated back into a magnetic pull that only that book could provide. Life had been rearranged, and in the back of his mind, that night, despite the suturing of his heart from the shattered mess it had remained. While he attempted to enjoy his girlfriend's return, the weight of guilt about Jonathan and his downfall was bearing down like a dagger into his brain. After they talked about their days, Daniel feigned exhaustion with a reluctance to truly dive into his day, knowing exactly how ludicrous it would sound. Sat down at the rustic oak table to have dinner, they joked and laughed in between their bites of food, just like old times. When they were finished, he pulled Rebecca in a deep, long embrace, kissing her deeper than even his memory could ever recall.

Rebecca, surprised, said, "Look at you kissing me like you missed me, you haven't kissed me like that since we met, well I'll see you in bed," she winked at him and flaunted her rear end playfully while she went off to the bedroom happily for the night.

It was not long before the guilt that had been slowly rising inside of him like an all-consuming tide of darkness, that Daniel found himself placing a telephone call to 1-800-AVARICE.

The dial tone rang twice, Veronica answered in her ultimate joyful tone. "Hello, Mr. Schmidt, are we enjoying the book so far? It's only one entry, but I do suppose it's a start, though maybe to more accurately record things, you should invest in a pen that works, I bet Rebecca has one."

A statement of facts that made Daniels eyes shoot wide open in a fearful display of disbelief as he pulled the phone away from his ear. He looked at the phone and then anxiously scanned the apartment with its girly décor— most likely Rebecca's doing. A room filled with different gold and purple knickknacks, incense holders, and even a chart about chakras and where they correlated to on the body. Though they weren't his main focus in the echo of the phone where Veronica prattled on describing his day in exact detail, his eyes couldn't help but behold how his home had changed as he felt his heart start thundering like a horse running a race around a track. That echo from the phone, wasn't doing anything to let loose its grip from Daniels' ability to speak. Everything was in such fine detail, even noting how he just had to have his face perfect at the beginning of the day.

Daniel finally stammered out, " how... how d-d-d-did you know any of that?"

Veronica's menace could be felt through the radio waves of the phone despite her joyful tone, " Mr. Schmidt, we keep close tabs on all of our friends for their wellbeing and ours."

Daniels mind jumped to wire taps, surveillance equipment, and even being on some sick game show. There were so many hoops his mind was passing through that he may have very well considered performing in the circus. Clearing his throat, "What is this? What are you? One minute everything is what I've always known, and the next, I'm suddenly a manager, and a guy that's been nothing but good to me is now a junkie and convict. I don't live where I used to, and I can't wrap my head around this."

Veronica retorted playfully, "Mr. Schmidt, first of all, your co-workers definitely got paid more than you. Jonathan got what he needed for his greed and cocaine use, now you can have anything you want, but you can't have everything you want. Someone, somewhere has to pay a price for what you want, didn't you read the instructions in the beginning?"

Daniel felt his annoyance needling into him, "You mean that shitty little poem, that wasn't a set of instructions, it wasn't even an introduction, I certainly didn't know I was going to ruin a whole person's life for what I wanted!"

This however prompted a much different voice than he was accustomed to hearing. This voice was dark and gritty like a rogue tide filled with ocean debris coming to flip everything upside down. "Mr. Schmidt, while I offer reasonable patron service, I'd advise you against your tone," said the voice, as it sank in tone like a ship in the night, ever deeper and more insidious to the point it reached the bottom of a demonic ocean. "Just because I am a pleasant voice on the other end of the phone, don't think for one minute I won't come to your home in Salem, New Hampshire in room 214 and rip the still beating heart out of your chest, just so I can make you eat it." Then abruptly the voice returned to its joyful British tone, "ok?"

Daniel's tongue was caught by the chain of events in a conversation. He found himself unable to form words as his heart pounded in his chest for a few moments.

Veronica beamed at him through the phone with a sickening artificial sweetness, "There, there Mr. Schmidt, I know I had to get a little serious on you there. It's ok the moment has passed and as long as you find a way to be pleasant with us, we will be pleasant with you, now take a deep breath, we're here to help all of our friends."

Coming back down to a workable anxiety, in an entirely different tone of voice that was verbally shaking out the words "ok,my mistake, Veronica, but I still have some questions about the book."

To which Veronica responded with the utmost joy yet again, "alright Mr. Schmidt, let's have them then,"

Daniel, finally winning in the search for his tongue, asking, "First, what are you?"

Veronica chuckled with maleficence at first but then gave up the answer. "Oh, Mr. Schmidt, we are watchers, we have been since before the flood, and we will be even after the fall of mankind, we don't sleep, we don't eat and everything you do, we see." Veronica paused only briefly and then continued. "After all, a friend in need is a friend indeed,"

Thoughts whirled around in Daniels head like a tornado. "So, what are you saying? That if I use this book, I'm going to lose my soul or something?"

An audible snort that became wicked laughter echoing through the speaker of the phone. Veronica was like a child thoroughly amused with their new toy on christmas morning, she let out a sigh that ended her laughter. She answered positively chipper, "No Mr. Schmidt. Technically, we don't deal in souls. Again you can have anything you want. However, your wants must be subtracted from the haves of others. The world needs to balance out essentially, like the ledger for a company."

The guilt of Jonathan that had been at the back of Daniel's brain, that deadly prion was finally coming full force, into a meltdown of guilt with his brain itself liquifying into tears that began streaming down his face. Through the tears he tried to choke back, he flipped open the book and said, "So, anything I want, anything at all I'll get? All I have to do is write it down and then everything will be balanced accordingly?" Daniel eagerly waited for the voice from the other end of the phone.

Veronica, after some moments of tepid silence finally brought the salve to his ears, "Absolutely, Mr. Schmidt, anything you want at all, just remember there is a price to be paid, but I think you understand that now."

As Daniel grabbed the pen, his thoughts centered on the heartbreak he had for years being repaired. But this was Jonathan and his price, as he scribbled on to the page of the open book: *I wish none of this had ever happened.*

Veronica on the other end of the phone giddily said, "Oh Daniel, after hundreds and thousands of millions of times, you'd think you'd learn to be more specific about a subject before you just go and write anything down." A final tear soaked confusion hit Daniel as the phone line went dead.

Daniel day finished in tears of guilt. He wandered into the bedroom, crawled into bed next to his only love. He embraced Rebecca tightly in his arms and drifted off to sleep. He'd never wish this burden on anyone.

* * *

The alarm clock rang out through the room with the sudden burst of Frank Sinatra I don't dance from the oldies station it had been set to from the day it was brought to the then-new home on that cold December day Daniel had moved into his apartment. Music which was almost entirely shrouded by the hammering rain coming down on that mid-April morning, Daniel had barely even heard it, even after it changed songs for nearly fifteen minutes. By the time, his bleary hazel wood eyes opened, it had made its way to the Chordettes hit song lollipop, another of his personal favorites. Ruffled red hair from the tossing and turning at night, anticipating today with all his excitement, he reluctantly despite his antsy nature, fell asleep. All due to last night's notification on his Samsung Galaxy phone which said that his shipment of books would be arriving today, fortunately, it coincidentally happened to be one of his days off. A decent turn of events since package theft was a little bit of a problem at his apartment complex, after all was said and done he pulled a decent amount of money at a locally owned restaurant as a cook. However, it would never be enough to cover all of his packages that had gone missing, to take that grand old second attempt of getting something he had paid for.

A pale white hand slathered with freckles slapped down on the off button of the alarm clock, the average yet gangly ginger featured man in his yogi bear pajamas arose from his full-sized bed decorated with a custom Deadpool comforter and matching pillowcase set. Passing by the modern styled bookshelves that lined his left wall, semi filled with books, more so lined with a particular series of comic books, mainly featuring the same peculiar character from his bed set that he had spent what seemed like an eternity collecting. Passing through the doorway with his hand accidentally brushing on the desk that also had his desktop computer he had custom-built; it was but a short distance to the bathroom in this one-bedroom apartment that he had finally made feel like home, despite the setbacks that had popped up along the way. Stopping in the view of the mirror to admire himself, the urge to stroke his ego was far too great, with Daniel speaking to his reflection in his oddly placed baritone voice, "you're getting older, but damn you still look good buddy," the tension down below suddenly reminded him that his bladder was the real reason that he had gotten up out of bed in the first place.

The time itself could not actually be told by the sun due to the weather going on outside, though it was his routine to get up at nine A.M religiously whether he was working or not, something he had learned in his early twenties. That way he could always have the time to get ready, he found it to be an insurance against the things that could happen, ever since Rebecca had left him and he went through that great depression, his routine he had set up years earlier was the anchor that kept that storm of his life from blowing him away. Finishing up with his bladder in an aim less than perfect, he had to bend down to wipe the seat. At that moment however, his lower colon suddenly didn't have a taste for Chinese food, the wonderfully bright idea he decided to have for his dinner last night. Slightly agitated he groaned, "I swear, why can't I ever just go to the bathroom all at once?" Taking a seat, he heard a knock at the door and simultaneously heard his phone on his nightstand go off with Captain America, "Avengers unite!" Which was followed up immediately by Daniel exclaiming, "god damn it!" It was a myriad of noise that came swirling into his ears at the most inopportune time, Murphy and his law always had a fine way of hitting him in the jewels, and it was always at the worst possible moment for it to occur.

Hurrying up with his surprise from last night's dinner, he washed his hands with the bar of dial soap sitting on the sink, drying his hands hastily with the brown hand towel hanging on the rack above the toilet, this was the first time in a while since he had been this excited. Turning both deadbolts and the lock on the handle of the door, he opened it up to the concrete pathway leading to his door in Salem New Hampshire, without a UPS man anywhere in sight. Looking down, his face lit up with joy as he bent down and picked up the box marked from Amazon.com and then a slight look of confusion as he suddenly noticed a much smaller box on the side of the door frame. The box was marked for his address in a plain brown cardboard box with a shipping label clearly marked for him and his address as he picked it up and inspected it somewhat thoroughly.

Taking both packages inside to his unremarkable kitchen table set and setting them down, he decided to go into the kitchen in the small one-bedroom grabbing a steak knife from a kitchen drawer that needed to find a sharpener. Diving into the amazon box first since that was what he was eagerly awaiting, he finally finished his collection of Victor Hugo by adding toilers at sea to the one of his many bookshelves in his bedroom. A first edition of the American Gods collection by Neil Gaiman and two Deadpool mint condition comic books he had been searching forever for, Deadpool kills the marvel universe and Deadpool issue number one.

Though if Daniel was honest with himself those comic book originals were about to go down in major value since they were about to be removed from their packaging and read about his favorite anti-hero that had always fascinated him since he was a teenager. However, curiosity was now eating Daniel even to the point where he openly asked himself the question out loud, "I wonder what is in the other box? I really don't remember ordering anything else that would have been shipped differently." Daniel made his way back to the kitchen to scan the box over once again, this time he noticed the name of the shipper as Avarice.inc as he remarked to himself somewhat bewildered, "sounds like some kind of investment company." Before using that same dull kitchen steak knife to open the box, to which he found another book, something that should have filled him with glee, instead it was replaced with morbid curiosity. Bound in black leather with gold brimming the edges of a book an inch and a quarter thick, it almost seemed like it could be some weird knock off of some religious text, maybe something belonging to a cult. He opened it up, finding the title page which read Avarice.inc a book for greed, followed by underneath it in italicized text the only book you will ever need, flipping beyond to the next page in his skeptical gaze. There appeared to be a poem of sorts, which read:

A friend in need is a friend indeed,
however, before you cultivate the seed.
Remember there is a price for greed,
From lucre to women or a stairway to heaven.

Greed is any strong want or need,
Which can bring despair the size of a sea.
Take great care of this book you received,
From fame to any setting be careful where you are treading.

After finishing the brief piece of poetry which to be honest, he was not even sure if he felt was all that great to begin with, he flipped to the next page finding it blank all the way to the end where he found the stamp of Avarice.inc followed by a one eight hundred number. "Alright well that was a creepy little piece of poetry," he remarked to himself as Daniel made his way to where his phone was set down on the nightstand in his room. "But that's alright, I am sure this was probably sent here by mistake, so I guess we will give them a call and get this all sorted out." Picking up the phone and walking casually back to the book he punched in the number after which he realized was quite literally 1-800-Avarice. A coincidence that brought a brief chuckle before mashing the call button while he sarcastically thought *oh how cute a custom telephone line.*

The phone rang twice with a quite pleasant and rather cute British female voice picking up on the other end, "hello, this is Veronica, thanks for calling Avarice.inc where a friend in need is a friend indeed and how is our friend Daniel Schmidt today?" Her voice echoed through the speaker holes of the phone reverberating off of his ear drum in such a manner that it was a stunning force, an auditory taser to his brain.

Daniel froze in place for a moment, stunned by a high voltage shock of unease. Wondering how in the world they could have known his name and then his brain finally clicked as he remembered the world of caller ID, which let him push out a relieved sigh followed by his answer, "yes veronica, I am actually calling about the book." With his New England accent growing thicker— as it always did around women, especially ones with candy toned voices, "I think I might have got this book by mistake."

Expecting a pause in the flow of conversation he was drastically surprised as Veronica responded instantly in her cheerful tones, "there are no mistakes at Avarice.inc sir, a friend saw that you were in need and asked that we send you our limited-edition book only for the choicest of audiences."

Growing a puzzled look on his face, Daniel responded in the most intellectual question he could muster, "uh . . . say what now?" Before correcting himself, "I guess what I mean to say is, I don't think I understand the book, there is a little poem in the front and then nothing, is it like a journal, some weird pseudo intellectual self-help book where you actually help yourself?" It almost felt like it should have been an easy question to answer in the grand scheme of things, but his brain seemed to be struggling like an overweight truck trying to roll up a hill.

Veronica's tone on the other end of the line never shifted from the ever-cheerful voice. She responded, "most of our friends find it to be the best self help book they've ever used; in fact, they even describe it as the most helpful book they have ever had." Though clear and concise with her words that softly cut through the question he had posed to her, it did nothing to erase the confusion growing on Daniels face–or for that matter even the heightening confusion in his mind. To which Daniel was about to shoot off another question to maybe gain himself some more clarity on the nature of the book, but Veronica cut him off with the answer, "just write what you want in the book and then you can have it, friend, it's that easy."

Daniel's brain finally seemed to click into place on the subject like two jigsaw pieces that finally got lined up. "Oh! So you mean like the law of attraction or that kind of thing? You know I've actually heard a lot about this, so it is like a self-help book," with his words rolling off of a sarcastic tongue.

Veronica with her permanent marker demeanor in its notes of cheerfulness, sweetly replied to him, "If that's how you'd like to see it, yes, it is like the law of attraction except if you write it in *this* book, you'll have much better results."

This kind of an answer gave Daniel the feeling that he was just going to go in circles with the woman, with that thought in mind he decided it was almost time to end the call, but not before the question sprang to mind. Who could have possibly thought he needed this pseudo intellectual garbage?

Veronica however, despite her witty english accent was quick on the draw like an old western gunslinger. She responded, "We don't give out friends' details sir. We appreciate you not asking, as part of our confidentiality and *yours*. Is there anything else I can help you with today, sir?"

Daniel was taken back a bit in surprise as though she had just read his mind to know what he was going to ask, logic however, came around the bend into the conversation where he figured it must have been a common question and brushed it off as just an interesting coincidence. There was not much else he could muster, in terms of trying to figure out this book, and so Daniel said, "no thank you I guess, that will be all."

Veronica replied absolutely chipper, "Anytime Mr. Schmidt, if you ever need help with the book, feel free to give us a call back at Avarice.inc. Where a friend in need is a friend indeed."

As the line went dead. Daniel thought, *well her customer service was great right up until the end there*. Taking another look in the book, he put it back on his kitchen table to keep the salt and pepper shaker company. "Alrighty then. *That* answered a lot of questions." Daniel rolled his eyes in dismay, being slightly weirded out by the entire conversation that had just occurred. Despite the oddity he found shortly thereafter his attention had shifted back toward ruining comic books that would ultimately be better off staying in the packaging. Hours passed as Daniel toyed away the day with all the new novelties in literature, but eventually the amusement faded, as it became overcast by his stomach growling as if it were the beginnings of a thunderstorm. Daniel put away his new sources of amusement and proceeded into the kitchen, since he had never truly learned to cook or portion for just one person, Hawaiian pork over rice that could have fed an army came out instead. Sitting down to eat at the table, right in his view was a steaming plate of sweet and savory sat down in the company of a book that in all of his wits paired off with his questions, he had absolutely zero answers for.

Daniel sat there as he slowly ate his food, feeling suddenly a vibe as if though the book itself was oddly staring out at him burning a hole into him with phantasmal eyes. Which was a very uncomfortable and beguiling feeling that made his skin prickle. Mid chew, Daniel said aloud "you know I suppose, I could use this thing as like a notebook or a journal."

After that jest, a statement of purpose for the book, the feeling seemed to slowly sink back into the depths, almost as if the book had been satiated by the notion that Daniel would find a use for it. After dinner he put the leftovers away into his apartment's supplied white fridge. Daniel immediately after began searching for a pen to at least be able to clip to the book, though it should have been easy. It quickly became an annoyance that culminated in him pairing the book with a pen he knew only worked when it felt like it. Grumbling while he shuffled off to bed for the night. He needed sleep. Tomorrow's shift lay just a few hours away, almost within his fingers' reach, shutting off the lights as he meandered toward his bedroom . Though probability with its percentages had spurned him in the search for a pen, fate had been kind. He'd spent the day in his pajamas, so no need to change. After he fell into bed, he set his alarm, plugged his phone in, and drifted to sleep.

The night passed by too quickly with the hours draining in a cyclone toward the drain. Daniel found himself having one of the sweetest of dreams. In it, he had become the manager of the restaurant where he worked and found himself reunited with Rebecca, the love of his life. But then the alarm clock went off, rudely blaring sounds from the oldies station.

Akten

"Hey, Serge!" Officer Cortez hollered in his Texas twang, a call that was easily heard throughout the Jackson Hole, Wyoming, police station.

The sergeant strolled out of his office to find one of his rookies holding a package with a note that read: *You know what to do with this,* scrawled in venetian red. At first, Sergeant Bellefonte wasn't quite sure what to make of it. He motioned for Cortez to bring the package and follow him to his office.

Sergeant Bellefonte radioed the K-9 unit with his gruff and naturally hoarse voice that echoed inside the small office. "Yeah, Lou. I need you to bring the dog up here, so he can sniff a package to see if somebody is trying to kill us."

The fifteen-minute wait seemed to drag on as they made small talk, chatting about the weather, sports, home life, and everything else in between, until the K-9 unit arrived. The German Shepherd, however, did not react with a single tell. The K-9 officer gave them the all-clear to open the package with a thumbs up gesture.

Sergeant Bellefonte breathed a sigh of relief and said, "Thanks for coming up here, Lou. It looks like this was a dud, thank God. Go ahead and get out on your route." The stone-faced sergeant with his stoic stature took out his Gerber pocket knife—the one he'd gotten the previous Father's Day from his ten-year-old little boy Michael. He sliced open the package and found a DVD in a clear jewel case, or at least that's what it looked like to his keen eyesight. He motioned for Cortez closer, and said, "I'm not really sure what's on this, but take it to evidence, to the DVD player and TV, see if it will play, if it's not some kind of recording we'll have to send it off. We don't want to get a virus on the station's intranet."

Officer Cortez found his way through the halls of the bland, run of the mill police station. He passed by offices and posters of missing people, before coming to the door of the stairwell, and jauntily headed down to the evidence room. He'd found himself in a good mood, since the skies were blue, and the sun shined brightly. His key unlocked the door, which opened to hordes of confiscated goods, from bags of cocaine to weapons of all shapes and sizes that were implicated in many a sordid dealing. Evidence from numerous cases had passed through the room. Nefarious activities arose like apparitions in the night only to disappear beneath the local police spotlight but would arise as the next day's gossip through the town's rumor mill, the stories wildly stretched out of proportion.

He set the DVD on a shelf to his right just as he walked in, and grabbed a tired, ancient flatscreen TV on a cart. Adjacent to it was the relic of a DVD player to match the TV. He rolled the combo around a corner of the L-shaped room so littered with evidence the wheels nearly locked up. He found his way back into the part of the basement that contained the evidence locker. Cortez squinted and scanned for an outlet. He shoved the cart into position and plugged in the TV and DVD player. He muttered to himself, "We are really going to have to clean this cage up one of these days." He snatched the DVD from the shelf, found a thinly padded chair, and settled himself in for the main attraction.

Finally feeling as though he had everything he needed at his disposal to see exactly what this may or may not be, he dragged the chair up to about three feet away from the TV. Cortez pressed the power button, opened the tray, pried the DVD from its plastic jewel case, the entire DVD system ran at the speed of a ninety-year old out for a walk at the retirement home. The screen switched to black for a few minutes even as the disc played. Officer Cortez nearly gave up on the hopes that this was some kind of video, before the screen finally shared the picture of a man he knew all too well. His finger jammed the pause to study the still grainy image that had exploded from the dark screen of the man sitting in a worn-out leather chair. While he knew the face, he just couldn't readily place it. He drifted back upstairs to the missing persons board and grabbed a poster.

The poster he grabbed off the wall pictured a forcibly retired park ranger that had gone missing in early 2017. His name was Joshua Almos, and even though Cortez was still relatively new to the area, this case stuck out like a sore thumb. Not because of his looks or anything specifically defining about him physically since he was essentially a run of the mill white male, but because this was the most interesting case he had ever seen go up on that board. The man had a reputation as a spectacular ranger but was forced into retirement with no clear reasoning. Then he vanished into thin air, not even his mother had an answer for where he might have gone. It was a strange case that had long held his attention. He was so engrossed at that moment he did not notice his sergeant down the hallway. He returned to the TV with the poster in hand, sat down on that uncomfortable steel chair, and pressed play, bringing the screen back to life.

"I used to be a park ranger at Yellowstone National Park back in 2016. I had ten years of service at that point, thought I'd make a career out of it, but let me tell you what changed my mind." His voice trailed off as though his mind was a computer struggling to boot the correct sequence of codes. He took a pack of Marlboro cigarettes out of his pocket, shook one out, and lit it up. He set the pack on a rustic wooden stand that had lost its lacquer, and sat on an old leather chair that had frayed where the hands rested. The man pulled a long drag off the cigarette before he began again. "You know I didn't use to smoke; shit didn't drink near as much as I do now either. But there are some things roaming around in this world that shouldn't be. I've got to make this goddamn video now, before they come and get me. Because now they know for sure that I know all their little secrets and what really causes the wildfires here."

An unnerving chill crept up Officer Cortez's spine like rising flood waters, brought on by the mannerisms of the man in the DVD. He remained focused on the screen as if reviewing security footage, watching intently, looking for clues. He paused the video again, certain in his own mind, that this was indeed the person who had been missing for more than three years. Finally, there could be some kind of resolution to all this mess, and just maybe the family would get the answers that they so desperately needed. The video recording itself would be a huge breakthrough in removing his poster from the wall.

Cortez resumed the video with even more attention to detail. This would prove to be one of the most entrancing days since joining the force. He would be the one to make a difference on a team that lacked proper affluence.

On the TV, the man took another hit from the cigarette. He grabbed a bottle of whiskey from the floor and drew a long pull. The lines on his forehead and his body language suggested he knew his time had grown short. His brown hair had gone speckled with gray, his sky-blue eyes sunk hollow in their sockets. One couldn't tell while he sat, but he was broad in the shoulders and if he stood up, he would be 5'10" with enough weight behind him that you'd find it a struggle to get him to the ground.

The man let out a nervous chuckle, and said, "You know, it was a day just like any other really. I got up and had breakfast at five a.m. Eggs, bacon, and toast, just like normal. I put on my ranger uniform and headed to work in my old jeep." His voice tapered off, for the briefest of moments, into a cross between the liquor and worry before he lit up again with his story. "It was the day before the lodgepole fire. I arrived and found Jerry was at his post. I had been making rounds all day when I got a call over the radio about some hikers that had gone missing, to put that on my list of things to do."

"Jerry said, 'Hey Joe, they may be out there in those volatile regions. It might be best to search for them while there's still daylight left to burn.' He was always trying to be helpful." The man on the video took another swig from the half gallon of Old Crow. Took it to the halfway mark. With sweat running down his face, he spoke again. "But that's why I've got to make this video, because, what I found out there. It just shouldn't exist, let alone those sick fucks who feed that thing!" He let out a winded sigh, evidence of a chain smoker. The whiskey he'd been downing like water colored his words. "I rode around on that little four by four Ranger. I covered hundreds of acres just looking for these people with sketchy details from Jerry, which at the time I thought was rather peculiar. The sun was starting to go down, and I was about to drive back to the station when I heard it. It was a chant coming from inside of the woods. It was like nothing I had ever heard before." He paused again. His face was a blur of confusion. He was drinking to gain the strength for what he meant to get across. Another swig of whiskey passed his Adam's apple before he finally set the bottle down.

"I couldn't understand what they were saying, but I parked the little ranger, and I started my trek through the trees like I was a soldier stuck behind enemy lines. Finally, I got to where I could hear them. I still couldn't understand what they were saying, but they were gathered around a geyser hole that I had never seen before in my ten years as a ranger. I thought I had been everywhere in the park."

After that sentence faint indistinguishable sounds could be heard coming from the outside, a myriad of baritone and bass just far enough removed that it could've been mistaken for loud vehicles pulling up on the outside of the property. "All right, I don't have a lot of time left. I found those two hikers. I couldn't save the woman," he said, as a lone tear strolled down his face. "But I drew my forty-five on that group of people standing around in white masks and robes that looked like they'd been dipped in blood. At first, they didn't notice me. They just kept chanting something about Akten. That's the only word I remember them using. Said it repeatedly." Sounds in the video from outside the cabin continued to escalate, growing louder and louder, as if someone had a hold on the volume knob of a speaker, twisting it higher as the seconds waxed on.

"I raised my gun into the air and popped off a round. They scattered like cockroaches when the lights were turned on. Each one running in different directions, scurrying away from a stone altar. The girl, she'd already had her throat slit and rib cage ripped open. It looked as if all her internal organs were missing. The man was still wrapped up in rope, bound and gagged like a freshly killed deer. I could tell he was still alive. Those cult fucks screamed from the woods, said I was making a mistake, that if I didn't let them finish this sick ritual that there would be hell to pay." The sounds from outside the cabin prompted another pause in the story. What sounded like a guttural hymn played on a loop encroached further into the video's audio, steadily seeping into the frames like black mold after a flood, spreading as it infected everything it met. The tired, half-drunk ranger rubbed his temples.

At that point in the video, the chanting could be heard just outside the cabin. As the man grabbed the camera with one hand, briefly removing himself from view, the sound of chafing could be heard as the chair, still in the frame, was dragged away. He turned the camera back on him and panned the cabin. Officer Cortez saw just how run down the place appeared while, at the same time, locked up tight. Wooden planks were sprawled across the windows and doors, blackened water stains colored the ceiling where the roof had leaked, floorboards jostled things into a hazard to trip over if a person was half awake. The long-tired breath washed over the next few frames, as the ranger composed himself, glimpsing the fact that time was no longer on his side to get his message out. He continued in the video in a rushed tone. "They were going on and on about a god of sorts in that pit, that if he didn't get his sacrifices, he'd start burning everything down to the ground.

"But I took that broken unconscious man, loaded him up in the Ranger, and took him back to that station. I tried to reach Jerry on my way back. I thought he had left, but Jerry was still there, and he told me." Audible banging cut him off mid statement. The source of it lay just outside of the frame of the camera. The cracking of timber ripped through the speakers of the TV. "I'm so sorry, whoever is seeing this. I tried to make it so people would know the truth." An audible thump was heard when the camera hit the floor. Dragging sounds echoed across the cabin. The video camera swung around to first reveal the retired park ranger with blood streaming down the side of his face, then outside to a busted wooden door. It flipped around to reveal someone in a venetian red robe, wearing a solid white face mask with a permanent smile. The person pressed their fingers against the alabaster lips of the mask making a *shh* sign, before fading to black.

At first, Officer Cortez thought it was over, before the video pulled up a shot of a stone altar surrounded by people clad in venetian red robes and white masks, chanting Cantus Nixferatu Akten in the woods. There on the slab lay the missing park ranger.

Bile churned in his stomach, as he watched a hand made of molten earth rise out of the hole near the stone altar. It grabbed the retired park ranger as he screamed in agony. Smoke billowed off the former ranger as the hand lifted him up and dragged him down into the hole. The camera panned back to another robed figure flashing the same *shh* gesture, before it cut to black and the DVD screen popping back on. Projectile vomit shot from the back of officer Cortez's throat. He exclaimed, "What the fuck was that?" He leapt from his chair. "I have to tell the sergeant about this." As his feet steadfastly moved, his brain ran at the speed of light through so many different thoughts. Everything about him was carried along on muscle memory. He was so focused on the thing he just witnessed. What *was* that? Why does it exist? Exactly how long had these things been going on with cult activity in Yellowstone National Park?

His thoughts were short lived. As he rounded the corner and headed up the stairs, Officer Cortez ran smack into the sergeant—and a group of men in venetian red robes. The men in white masks stood menacingly behind him. The light from the stairwell exposed the *shh* gesture—fingers against lips—except for the sergeant who conveniently did not wear a mask. It was a deadlock, a standstill, where time appeared to slow down to creep, a trickle of seconds, still frames that spelled out things as obvious as they were. A terrible situation of being outnumbered, followed by the implications that he should have never been down there acting as Dudley Do-Right of the force. He'd only meant to make an impression. One that would lead to him being trusted with more, so that he could move up the ladder, and maybe do the things he dreamed of accomplishing.

Cortez snapped back into the present.

Bellefonte chimed with criminal glee, "Oh, George . . . how are we going to fix this?"

Cortez found his tongue tied in the standoff between him and the group that blocked his way with a barricade of people, that instead of shuffling toward him, backed up and gave him and Bellefonte more space. The abnormally dark hallway was quiet. Everything thickened with suspense, with the way the elements mixed in that exact moment in time. *Sinister* was the word that Cortez sought inside of his mind. It was too much of a coincidence the way this had played out from the very beginning of this little expedition. Deep down he had constructed the pieces inside his mind. They all fell into place thanks to this standoff. The mystery needed just one final clue to put everything together.

His tongue loosened from the binding that held it down. As he eagerly scanned the room for a way out of the situation, he said, "Hey, Serge. Fancy meeting you here like this. Did you find something else for me to go do?" It was an attempt to play it like he hadn't discovered what was on the DVD. A play at ignorance seemed the only way to go since all his exits were cut off by the palisades of venetian red.

Sergeant Bellefonte chuckled, and said, "Listen, you had a good run, kid. This can go easy, or it can go hard. If you let it go easy, you won't feel a thing." He offered a proposition that held no favorable alternatives, no silver lining.

Cortez fired back, "I really don't know what you're talking about, Serge. I went down there and watched a video for about an hour, but it's just a black screen." He paused, then asked, "Who are your friends, Serge? Isn't it a bit early for Halloween? Also, did we lose power? It's awfully dark in here for the middle of the day."

Playing the part of the fool seemed like a good card to try to play out of this hand, really it was the only card on the table he could try to play. The white masks offered their insidious smiles calling his bluff in silence as he and Bellefonte locked eyes.

Bellefonte said, "Listen, Cortez, you and I both know what you saw. You know who they are. I'm trying to tell you; you don't want to make this harder than it has to be." That's the funny thing about stupidity though, you can only play that card when there's a big enough buffer to supply some cushion between the known and unknown variables of the world.

"Come on, Serge," Cortez said. "I'm getting married in two months. We both know I'm not going to step out of line without your approval. Hell, didn't you tell me to knock it off, that I wasn't in the academy anymore?"

Bellefonte sneered beneath an unruly tangle of gray hair. "You know, Cortez, I think we can work something out. You're not going to like it. Hell, I didn't like it at first, but I knew that it was necessary." Bellefonte waved his hand, directing the cultists to clear the hall. Then he motioned for Cortez to follow behind him, which got his back away from being against the wall. Cortez followed close behind Bellefonte with an eagerness to listen to anything he had to say to escape the least-favored scenario. "There are many necessary evils in this world. We still use fossil fuels even though we know it's killing our planet. We persist in meddling around with nature even though the natives who were here thousands of years before us knew better. There is a balance to everything." At the end of the hallway, as they reached the main lobby, the lights snapped back on.

The cultists had all vanished into the ether.

Bellefonte said, "You're going to make a drug bust that ends in suicide by cop—if you get my drift."

Cortez saw a way out of this mess. "I'll do it, Serge. But I must know, what was that thing?"

Bellefonte didn't bat an eyelash at the question. He simply explained, "It's something the natives used to keep quiet before colonialism almost wiped them out. We don't know if it's a god or not, but it has the power of one. If it loses its cool, the United States is more than likely never going to recover."

Cortez's thoughts of fleeing became muddled with the question of *does the end really justify the means?* It was for the good of everything, wasn't it? The weight of it all held his feet to the floor like glue. It was a scenario of what if? Defeat slid from his brain to his mouth; the thoughts of running and never looking back faded from his mind. "All right, Serge, I'll do it. But this better be as great an evil as you make it out to be."

That evil sneer spread across Bellefonte's face like a black Cadillac on a slow creep through a residential neighborhood. "Bold of you to assume you have a choice, Cortez. Now go out there and let's keep a vitriolic, living breathing volcano god—for lack of a better title—satiated down in the depths of Yellowstone Park."

Cortez nodded as he begrudgingly stepped into the world to accomplish the thing that would cause him to lose sleep. He targeted criminals that would later become sacrifices. Some were junkies, some murderers, and plenty of gangbangers that happened to be passing through. At least that's what the reports all read. I could go on about the way things played out for Cortez and his family, how he had a family, got promoted, and ultimately did so many great things for the community that he helped protect. But I'm afraid that it's about time for the ritual sacrifice, and I need to put on my robe and mask for the preparation of the ceremony. But don't you get any wise ideas.

We can find you too, wherever you are. It would be a terrible shame if one day your family couldn't find you, then it turned out that you just happened to get lost on a hike in Yellowstone Park. After all, people go missing all the time in national parks. Just look it up. It's quite a conundrum. Maybe we were involved with many of them and maybe we weren't. Akten isn't the only elemental god in North America, but he is the most unstable. I hope you've enjoyed this special peek into our world. Just remember now, you'd better *shh.*

Adoption

As the sun began rising over verdant fields, peeking in through windows of the homes they were plastered upon, a breeze sighed that rustled the grass swaying calmly in a gentle rocking motion. A melancholy gust that wouldn't have blown if it wasn't commanded to do so by the upper atmosphere. The roar of engines echoed as people began leaving for work on the Friday of that May morning. Sounds that were of no consequence to the ears of someone jutted awake by the screeching of an alarm clock that had been forgotten about, a usual occurrence for the days off that was always followed by the thoughts of, *why didn't I turn that off?* Moaning in response to the clock with its incessant chatter, Andrea wearily opened his eyes and saw the brand new one-hundred-gallon tank. Groggy from the depths of middle age that had seeped into his bones from years out on tour in different parts of the world, despite the annoyance, it wouldn't have mattered if the alarm was set or not, he would have simply gotten up anyway.

Through the moaning and groaning, the usual self-talk of why he was up this early would have still played out in a typical fashion. After all, as they say, old habits die hard. Speaking of old habits, it was a sentiment shared by someone else in the house, with the sounds of purring that could be heard as a calico cat nuzzled up against his feet at the end of the bed, rubbing his eyes with his right hand since his other arm was still tucked up underneath his pillow. Forcing a stretch as he lazily moved one leg at a time to touch the linoleum floor, coldness jolted through the bottom of his feet that made the rest of him react in a very similar fashion that finished itself off with a shiver through his spine. He sat on the edge of his bed, glanced at his cat Frisco, and muttered in a raspy voice, "I suppose it's about time to get something to eat." Wincing from the soreness, football took more of a toll on him at age thirty-five than he was willing to admit. He just didn't recover as well anymore, and like always, they didn't really follow the touch rules to a T when they played ball.

Shuffling his feet that he barely even made the attempt to raise up from the floor, he made his way into the kitchen that was otherwise unremarkable aside from a new stainless-steel fridge that his landlord had so kindly installed since the other one made a solid attempt at being a sauna. Bending down to the cupboard next to the fridge, he opened it up in such a way that it startled the cat, who had been following him as if he was tied to his leg with a leash since he left his room. He grabbed a bag of Friskies and poured some into the cat's bowl, which left him without his one cat entourage who clamored behind him for the feast. Continuing his shuffle into the bathroom, he made himself ready. Stripping down for a shower, revealing all the scars of his previous exploits from being overseas on deployment in the desert, it was a collage of bullet wounds that had been covered up. Long lines from a fragmentation grenade that he had barely thrown back in the nick of time while trying to save his battle buddy, who, at that moment, had been shocked that an insurgent threw a grenade rather than having the entire place booby trapped, which was their modus operandi.

All these scars dredged up memories that on occasion still flooded his mind with the filth-covered stains of desert winds. It was nothing in comparison with the much more wet septic wound that never seemed to heal with his ex-wife who decided to move on before he was dead. Sometimes it still brought tears to his eyes, which made him question so many things that he could have done differently, but largely he had carried on from the entire ordeal and made jokes about keeping the cat. He was in dire need of those small victories at the time when it seemed as though everything had been sucked into the abyss, and instead of being with someone new, he devoted his time to work, and found contentment with the cat. Work, and that cat, ultimately seemed like a better alternative than to ante up and lose everything again. Though recently, he had taken up a fascination with Koi fish and had one set to pick up today. It was interesting, since he hadn't really considered himself much of a fan of fish. But on one of his many tours, he happened to be stationed in Japan, and always found Koi to be a beautiful fish. Often, he would take the time to feed them while he talked to the wind as if it could respond.

The fascination that he thought had died when he left Japan, instead of lying in a morgue as some decaying memory, it had resurfaced when the pet store owner told him that now he could start getting a new kind of fish on special order. Of course, it perked Andrea's curiosity, eventually though in that catalog he found a beautiful calico painted fish, that he made jokes about with his friend Josef who ran the pet store, that it would match the cat. Coming back down to earth from his transcendental trip, down the different memories that ended on a happier note, he found himself finishing up getting dressed in an old Black Sabbath t-shirt, and jeans with a hole around the left knee. He slid on a pair of old sneakers that were beaten down and way past their prime, like a boxer that didn't know how to retire, which he didn't even bother unfastening to get on. He picked up the keys off the foliage-colored tiled countertop to his charcoal black nineteen-eighty-nine mustang with the five point zero engine he was so proud of. He naturally went creeping out the door so that hopefully the cat wouldn't decide to find the outside world more interesting in contrast with the buffet of cat food it was enjoying, it wouldn't have been the first time Frisco had tried to make a break for it.

Sauntering out to his car in a lackadaisical way, unhindered by the norms of a work schedule that generally had him in more of a rush to go down to the plant, he felt like he might be missing something as he patted himself down, realizing that he had in fact taken everything including his phone. Shrugging it off as a pin drop of paranoia in the larger scheme of things, he plopped down into his mustang, and started it up. He felt the custom cam job rumble through his ears. Dropping the floor shifter into reverse, he started out of his neighborhood with the Godzilla-like roar of his muffler. It was the small comforts that he could afford that made him smile these days. After fifteen minutes stuck in traffic listening to the soundtrack of classic rock that endlessly blared out the windows, he pulled up to the strip mall with its faded parking lines that, at this point, people just took turns guessing. He'd been here to visit Josef often enough to memorize where the potholes were. Taking a deep breath, he turned off the car and killed the radio that was blaring Guns 'N Roses through his custom speakers.

Swinging the door open in an otherwise empty parking lot, he manually locked his car and strolled up to the shop door which chimed that cheap dime store ring, followed by the serene tones of Josef greeting him with, "Long time no see." The old, tired man followed it up with a chuckle, since Josef knew that was anything but the truth. He hit back again quickly, saying, "I think I know what might have brought you here."

Scrunching up his sixty-three-year-old face in an attempt at pretending to remember, Andrea, spat back playfully, "Don't play like you can't remember, old man. You might be ugly, but you're not forgetful." He followed Andrea walking up and setting his keys down on the counter, as he wiped the corners of his eyes which still had the crust from sleep.

The playful old man quipped, "Oh, but even for sixty-three, I'm still not near as ugly as you, anyway, yeah, yeah. I know what brought you in here. You've been waiting for a hot minute now." Josef disappeared like a ghost in the morning sunlight into the back area of his quaint little store. It was fitting, since he was lucky to be one-hundred and ten pounds soaking wet—if you turned your head too fast you would miss him.

Which left Andrea to wander around the shop eyeing the exotic birds that he took turns trying to talk to in a voice usually reserved for animals and babies. The birds were oddly quiet for a change of pace, much to his surprise. The dogs, on the other hand, seemed to be acting like their normal selves running around energetically, and playing with each other in the big kennel. A Saint Bernard paired off with a cocker spaniel in a game of tug of war for a comical match up. Cats were sleeping in their own little secluded area, ball pythons steadily testing their luck against the tightness of the lid on top of their terrariums in a game to see exactly how strong they were, and what curiosity could do to let them out. Suddenly, he was hit by the jolt of Josef's voice cutting through his wandering focus of all the different pets splayed throughout the store. Granted, the Saint Bernard was Josef's dog.

"Trying to add more to the collection to match the cat, hmm?" Josef chuckled at his own joke, as most elderly men tended to do in their golden years, not taking life too seriously anymore.

Andrea smirked and retorted, "You know I like to look around, but I don't know. You got any calico-colored snakes or birds? Don't answer that. I know you'll find one somewhere."

Josef hoisted up the bag that held the calico fantail Koi fish. It seemed like it was floating off the bottom of the bag, as if it were an ethereal being, until it flicked its fins calmly. Andrea beamed at the sight of such a beautiful fish, its color was immaculate he thought, as he reached into his back pocket, and pulled out the beat-up leather wallet that looked like it was dragged across the road at sixty miles an hour. He handed his debit card to Josef.

The old man whimsically chimed in again, like he was talking to one of his grandchildren that just got a birthday present from him. He said, "Now, you know you have to let the bag rest in the water first before you just drop the fish in there, right?"

To which Andrea grew a little bit exasperated, hinted at by a little bit of a deeper breath than usual. He replied, "Yes, I know, Josef. I wouldn't have picked this if I didn't bother to read up just a little bit."

Josef shrugged his shoulders, said, "Easy, tiger. It's just a reminder, if you know, but umm, shouldn't you grab some fish food for the little guy?"

Which made Andrea smack his head. "God almighty. I guess you're right. They won't make it that long without that, will they?"

As he meandered over to where the pet food supplies were in the little store, where indecision took over, his eyes blankly scanned the different types of food for fish.

The pause seemed to call on Josef in his commentary. "If you aren't sure, just grab the can with the koi fish on it that says *pellets*. It might say blood worms or something of that sort on it."

Andrea bent over and pulled up a can of koi fish pellets with the picture of a koi fish on them, just like Josef had said.

Upon seeing Andrea's head pop back, Josef rubbed his forehead in a sarcastic fashion with a silly look on his face. "I thought you said that you had done your research, buddy. And here we are with you staring off into space, for fish food. God, what am I going to do with you kids?"

Walking back at the same pace, ribbing back and forth, the two continued on like kids on the playground. "Listen, you can't rush a man on such an important decision. It's for the health of the fish. It's not like we're talking about something trivial like my ex-wife." The comment itself almost made it seem like it was going to bust Josef's hernia from the amount of laughter that roared out of him.

Andrea put the can on the counter, said, "So, I guess now you can go ahead and run my card." He was shaking his head over the absent-mindedness that had somehow crawled into his mind, as Josef went ahead and ran the card through the machine, tearing off the small piece of paper that Andrea signed for everything.

With the payment made and the receipt handed back to him, Josef piped up, "I have an old story about these koi fish, if you have a minute. It's interesting because around the world people have similar stories about the theme they center around."

However, Andrea hadn't eaten before he bothered to leave, a mistake that was hammered into him by the emptiness in his stomach, as he was entirely too focused on making sure his cat Frisco ate instead, as well as not letting him dart out the door into the wild blue yonder.

Which became apparent to Josef as well, since his stomach had begun growling just before he spoke up. "Actually, I think I need to get something to eat, but I will definitely take the time to catch up with you soon."

Andrea took his debit card after the purchase and shoved it haphazardly into his wallet, before subsequently ramming that old broken-down wallet back into his pocket.

Grabbing the plastic bag with the koi fish nestled inside, he shoved the can of pellets into his right front jean pocket and waved his goodbye, snatching his keys off the counter. Trotting away giddy and hungry, he pushed open the door, setting off the chime. The sun had come to smack him in the face, nearly blinding him from the sudden burst of light, involuntarily making him squint as he made the way back to his car which luckily wasn't all that far in relation to the store front. Swiftly unlocking the car door, he opened it with his free hand, feeling the sudden rush of collected heat flooding out of the car like a swarm of angry wasps, hot enough in such a short period of time that he needed to let it slowly roll out for a minute or two. After letting the heat escape, he then leaned forward into the Mustang and set the koi fish down carefully in the passenger seat. In the process of setting down the koi fish, that gentle breeze from earlier that had been present all day, picked up into a gust making the door slam into his backside, which sent a disgruntled wave that washed away the giddiness. On top of that, hunger that had been swirling in his stomach, made itself known. As he climbed into the car and tried to take the passenger-side seat belt to fasten the fish bag in place, he eventually was successful with a wrap around the bag itself.

Once securely in place, he was off like a rocket back to his two-bedroom home that did not have to be two bedrooms, considering the circumstances. He was held up by the same traffic that prevented him from getting to the store in the time frame he wanted to begin with. After the short ride that felt longer due to the lack of food and agitation from the incident with the door, the Mustang sat parked on the heavily cracked concrete. He undid his restraints around the bag he had tied up, which still amazed him that they had held for the entirety of the ride. Grabbing it gently, and opening his car door while fighting the wind, Andrea pulled the key out of the ignition while holding the door with his left leg, making the firm judgment call that it would work out better rather than getting hit in the shin. Locking it up as he went back to his front door, where he unlocked the next door in his journey, and proceeded to the fish tank, abruptly shutting the door behind him, so that the damn cat wouldn't try to pull a Shawshank redemption. He made his way to the fish tank, tossing his keys on the kitchen table as he passed by, taking the fish food out of his pocket as he held them both into the bedroom. He placed the koi fish in its separated bag of water on top of the fresh aquarium water for the adjustment period to begin so that the fish wouldn't go into shock, setting the fish food on the cabinet inside the stand, as he plugged in the filtration system and air stones.

Back in the kitchen, he rummaged around in the lower cabinets and pulled out a pot to make spaghetti. Tossing the spaghetti on the counter, after he filled up the pot with water, he poured in Himalayan pink salt. He turned on the large burner to get a jump start on the spaghetti and grabbed a smaller pot to make some of his own sauce. He lost himself in cooking as he so often did. Cooking had never been a chore for him. He always found it freeing in the way that he could just experiment and come up with new combinations to tantalize his taste buds. As the food was nearly done, he heard a loud bang, and his cat hissing like the wood in a wildfire. He dropped what he was doing and burst into his bedroom to find the torn open bag with shreds of plastic strewn about as if a tornado had blown through.

The Cat shot out of the room like a ballistic missile as though it had been smacked with the saucepan that he had just been cooking with. As he eagerly scanned the room, he found the fish underneath the nineteen-fifties style nightstand. He rushed over, pulled it out, saw broken skin on its back with some exposed flesh. He did the only thing he knew to do and dropped the fish into the tank, where it appeared to be stunned. After a few moments, it began swimming again. Frantically, he pulled his phone from his front right pocket, searched for vets in the area, and determined which ones either could or couldn't work on a brand-new fish. Finally, he got a hold of a vet. The encouragement on the phone was overwhelming. He listened as the vet told him how the fish could die from bacteria under the cat's nails alone—never mind the damage caused to the fish from the attack. With the phone pressed to his ear, he returned to the kitchen in search of a Ziploc bag. He combed through each drawer like the dragline on a search party for a missing kid, until he found a box in one of the middle drawers.

With a Ziploc bag in hand, he rushed back to the tank, scooped out a healthy amount of water, and then coerced the fish inside with the help of a small net. With the fish in its temporary home on the countertop, Andrea poured the sauce on top of the spaghetti like a Jackson Pollock painting. He flung the pan in the sink, where it hit with a resounding clang. It all didn't really seem to matter since he was in such a hurry. Sliding out a plate from one of the upper cupboards that would be placed on top of the pot with his creation, it also got tossed in the fridge just as it was, figuring that ultimately, while not ideal, it was better than nothing at all. Eventually, he'd be able to eat at some point. He snatched up the fish bag, made his way to the kitchen table to retrieve his keys, and began a long journey to the vet. The fish had to be lightly cauterized.

The vet explained, "Be very careful, that she may not want to eat for a day or so, but that was normal since the fish was so highly stressed."

The bright rays of the early morning had then turned into the amber glow reminiscent of a fire signaling the shift into the afternoon. He jostled with keys once more to go back into the house, exhausted from a day that was supposed to be just a normal kind of day tinged with excitement.

The groans could be heard from his car while he rubbed his temples, with a breath as though he were a locomotive pushing out steam. His eyes settled on the fish in his passenger seat in a bag the vet had provided.

He said, "I hope you appreciate this."

He took the bag less energetically than before, so that he wouldn't lose something else that started to bring him joy. He softly made his way inside the house, back to his bedroom, before gently setting the fish back in the water in the new bag that the vet had so graciously provided for yet another adjustment period. Walking back out into the kitchen somberly, he pulled the pot from the fridge and made a plate of spaghetti that spun around in his 900-watt microwave for two minutes. Grabbing a fork out of the drawer beside where the Ziploc bags were kept which was a much neater space, the decision crossed the forefront of his thoughts to eat on his bed where he could watch the fish, making sure that it was undisturbed this time. Which turned out to be a good thing too, he already saw the cat creeping back which had a penny flung next to where they were to scare them off. Finishing his plate, and finally able to release the fish into the water after all it had been through, he went to stow away his dishes in the sink to be washed up tomorrow morning. Heading out into the living room he sank into his favorite recliner, turning on the tv to watch Netflix, forgetting about a more exhausting day than when he went to work.

Several hours flew by in a matter of moments as show after show streamed through in seamless binge watching. Somewhere in between the snacks and drinks, the cat had forgiven him about the penny, finding his way to be rubbing up against Andrea's legs. Deciding to officially call it a day, he got up from the chair begrudgingly with a groan, like that of an oak tree pressed by the wind, making his way to the bathroom where he stripped down and washed vigorously with water hot enough to scald even the heartiest of demons. Stepping out into the thick fog from all the steam of the shower, he went to his bedroom robed with a towel around himself, getting dressed into boxers, and another band t-shirt while he silently contemplated such a busy day with misfortune at one of the earliest turns. Covered up enough to be presentable in the broadest of ways, he traipsed back out into the kitchen where he grabbed a glass from the cupboard, pouring a glass of water from the kitchen sink to take his medicine on the counter that largely alleviated his PTSD. Swallowing everything down in one solid gulp was a big relief, he always hated it when it felt as if the pills got stuck in his throat, finally it was off to bed where he crawled in looking at the koi fish across from him to see that it was swimming around just before closing his eyes.

Tossing and turning at every inopportune moment in the middle of the night, he rolled over and felt his hand slide over something while his eyes weakly opened, revealing to his sight a flawlessly beautiful cerulean woman staring at him. Jolted awake as if electricity had just been shot through him like he was hooked up to the electric chair, he fell out of bed with a crash and quickly grabbed his revolver that was holstered beneath the nightstand. After all, God may have made men, but Samuel Colt made them even, his revolver in his hands steadfastly got aimed at the spot on the bed where the woman was as he sprung back up from the floor. The spot appeared to be vacant as he caught his breath that, for a moment, had been wildly running out of control, lowering the gun as he slumped down on the floor. Looking underneath his bed and there she was, as he pointed, and the click could be heard from an empty chamber that was left that way just in case there was some mistake. A contingency that always felt necessary considering things could always be an illusion that alluded to something else entirely in the cases of if they were supposed to be there or not.

With the cylinder turning as the two stared at each other, her with a smile so serene, and him with his anxiety rapidly rising, he exclaimed, "The next one's live, so you'd better tell me who you are, and what you're doing here."

The sky-blue woman slid out from the bed and gestured to the fish tank almost to grant the appearance as though she couldn't speak. The tank itself, which appeared to be empty, filled the room with the allure of mystery. The more she slid out from underneath his queen-sized mattress, the more it became apparent that not only was she nude, but her body was something that sculptors would have wished to engrain in the sands of time forever. She slowly turned her backside to him showing the wound up by her shoulder blades, contorting in almost an unnatural manner, yet still within the realms of what could be considered humanly possible. He lowered the gun with it steadily falling in slow motion. His brain struggled to keep up with the situation, lacking the computational power to put everything together, glancing between the tank, and her in a game of visual insanity, continuously expecting a different result, almost stuck in a loop.

Her lips finally parted into a divide that finally contained syllables and said, "I just wanted to say thank you . . ." with a shy gesture as she inched closer to him.

A quiver rolled up his arms, sending his hairs into needle points. In a bout of nervousness, he hadn't quite felt before in his life, he looked at her as he hardened his resolve, and said, "Prove it." Unfortunately, the answer that came raining down on him wasn't what the foresight in him was anticipating for the challenge he just submitted to her. As bones twisted, skin folded, size kept reducing into a dark grotesque painting brushed before his very eyes, his stomach churned at the visual display presented to him. The collage of sound came together like a mob boss's vendetta against his ears. The sounds of cracking and sloshing, like a ship punctured by its own mast, the sound so reminiscent of a wild sea creature that was gnashing its teeth down onto a boat of unsuspecting fishermen, or so he imagined. Suddenly, there was a small koi fish flopping around, and even though he saw it, his brain was at a loss for words as the canvas remained blank. He was stuck like an ant in a glue trap that didn't have the heart to gnaw off its own legs to get out of it without being completely stunned. The vapors of being aghast fluttered inside his lungs. He felt his tongue caught in a vise. He set the gun off to the side to allow himself to pick up the koi fish and slide it back into the tank. Finding the fish food, he gave the koi fish as he began to wonder what he just saw, as it swam around, eating much sooner than the vet gave any kind of inclination to.

Did he just have a psychotic episode? It wouldn't have been the first time that something like that had occurred to him, but if that's what it was, where did it come from? His mind was like a dam, releasing thoughts with it trying to contain the situation and prevent a breach. A blank stare locked onto a Koi fish as it swam around continuously eating the food he had poured over the surface of the water. The sound of the air bubbler created the white noise that held the whole situation together as a distraction to what he had just witnessed. After placing the canister of food beneath the aquarium tank, he was more than willing to write this off as a touch of insanity.

He picked up the gun, put it back into its holster underneath the drawer after winding the revolver back to the empty chamber, crawled into bed, and covered up. He tried to still his mind, though it seemed to be a rather fruitless effort on his part in terms of trying to produce the kind of still water one usually needs to successfully fall asleep.

His mind with its thoughts continued as he passed out into his chaotic dark dreams, where he saw the same woman, her mouth filled by angler fish teeth devouring the heart of a man with a sickeningly tight grin. It was enough to make him jerk upright in a cold sweat. The monster movie that played in his head was certainly a variety of messed-up he had never seen before. Usually, it was something that happened when he was overseas, distant shores of memories on repeat. He looked over at the tank to see that the koi fish was occasionally flicking its fins to stay afloat, otherwise there was nothing too wild playing out before his eyes. Satisfied with reality shifting back to where it truly belonged, somewhere in the realms of mundane powdered with solitude, those eyes wandered back over to the phone on his nightstand, he pressed the power button seeing that it was eight-thirty-seven a.m. A whole twenty-three minutes before his alarm went off, a situation that worked well for him as he didn't know exactly how much more of that dream he could possibly stand. He had seen some wicked things, but watching another creature devour a man's heart right in front of his own eyes in a voracious display, spraying blood all over its mouth, sent his stomach spinning like a fan on high.

He got out of bed, nowhere near as lazy as the day before, and strode out to feed the cat, which oddly didn't greet him in its usual loving fashion. It seemed tired and less playful with as much charm as a drunk man in a mall. Reluctantly the cat ate its food, though Andrea could tell that it was most certainly not happy about anything this morning, a message that became clear when he bent down and tried to pet him. The cat hissed like a geyser in a national park letting loose its pressure with a tower of steam, which made Andrea remark unamused, "Well, ok then. Be like that, I guess." He decided to check the mail since he had completely forgotten about it the day before, what with all the excitement. He threw on a pair of pants that should have been tossed long ago, due to all the rips from the many years of use. But he never could part with them. They were a perfect fit. He put on some shoes and opened his front door. He was immediately greeted with flashing red and blue lights that lit up the neighborhood from two houses down, like dual-colored fireflies floating. His eyes caught an ambulance loading up a covered gurney. He shook his head with a glint of sadness in his eyes. Suddenly, his eyes shot open as he remembered the dream. Inside his chest, his heart swelled as it rocked back and forth like a madman in a padded cell from the dark traumatic scenes that his mind tried to let loose into the wasteland of forgotten dreams.

He turned around from his mailbox and retreated from the situation at hand. Back inside, he prepared for a shower and set out new clothes for the day, ones that possibly weren't so worn. He walked back inside into the quaint little bathroom, turned on the hot water, got undressed, and didn't bother looking at his reflection today—not that it was something that brought butterflies to his stomach anyway. Out of the corner of his eye, as he stepped beneath the water, he caught the cerulean woman staring, smiling, as if she saw something she wanted to buy. Her eyes fixed on him like a different kind of predator than the rendition he saw in his dreams. A feeling grabbed hold of him with a sensation of electricity over his skin, prickling his nerves like cactus needles diving in from an accidental bump, jarring in the most unsubtle of ways. He scrubbed and washed clean, feeling the eyes on him, the woman smiling so contently. He felt unhinged, as if his medicine had stopped working without putting in a two-week notice. He finished his creep-filled shower, got out and dried off.

The faint sound of a giggle chortled from the steam-filled bathroom. A sensual voice followed, asking, "You'll take care of me, won't you?"

He tried his best to shake it off, ignoring it while putting on his clothes. He turned around to go to the living room, since the last place he wanted to be was the room where his sanity seemed to be unraveling.

He sat down in his favorite chair and turned on his TV with the remote to get his mind off where it had been wandering for it to land on the news. One couldn't go wrong with the news. Sure, it was depressing, but most of the time it wasn't your own sad story. They were discussing how his neighbor had died of a very violent heart attack. Paramedics who were interviewed said that his heart ruptured with so much force that there was no hope even if they were there the instant it happened. This news made him shed his anxiety like a winter coat. Finally, something that made a whole lot more sense than what had been going on. He closed his eyes and leaned his head back against the recliner chair. He muttered, "I'm getting too old for this." When the cat came and rubbed up against his legs, he reached down to pet it as it purred and bunted against him. Talking to Frisco, he said, "I think I made a mistake. I don't know exactly what's going on, but I don't think we were meant to have a fish." He continued petting the cat before it abruptly took off with a sudden burst of speed and began playing with a toy. He got up as well, shut down the TV in a fluid motion of rising and hitting a button on the remote that he sat back down in its spot. "I have to get out of here for a while," he said to the cat. "Be good for Daddy, Frisco." He went searching for his keys, forgetting where he had stashed them the day before.

He stepped into his shoes. The only sound carrying on through the house was that of the cat playing with its toy that had a bell on the inside of it, which gave him comfort from the things that had been going on very recently. He slipped out the front door and made his way to the Mustang.

He followed his normal procedure of making sure the cat didn't escape the house. After locking the house, he rubbed an eyelash out of his eye and unlocked his car. He fell into the seat, closed the door, started the engine, shifted into gear, and headed off to a diner for breakfast, maybe some coffee. The idea of distance right that second also gave him the idea he could clear his mind with food he didn't have to make. The dark circles under his eyes were like welts from an abusive love, highlighted to other people who would indirectly do their best to make sure that he didn't forget his night as he entered the diner. A concerned look here, a hushed comment over there—even the man that he passed on his way inside asked him if he was ok.

The waitress came to take his order with a concerned look in her eye. She said, "Didn't sleep so well last night, Hun?" An innocent enough question.

He looked at her in a somber way, replied, "No, I didn't have a good night, to say the least." This ended his social interactions—aside from ordering his food and paying.

The last interaction at the diner, which was little more than basic formalities of wishing each other a good day, certainly didn't overwhelm him with the feeling he was going to have one, as things got strange very quickly. Somberly, he dragged his feet toward home. He hadn't really slept that much lately. He dropped into the Mustang, which still felt like his greatest comfort. It wasn't as if he really wanted to have a day out on the town, painting it red, as the expression goes, to be around people. He'd probably flare up since he was already having symptoms. He slammed gears as he made his way home, rolled down the window just to feel the breeze circulate through the car as he breathed deeply and finally felt like he had some steady place in his own mind, a thorough place to stand. He judged the events that made him question his perception. He pulled into his driveway and let out one last deep breath, rolled up his window, got out of the car, and realized how much the wind and the ride itself as well had calmed him down. It made for quite a pleasant surprise as he approached the front door, finally feeling relieved as if the world had been lifted off his shoulders for a moment. Maybe the food helped, too. It seemed a hearty combination of things that gave him the sanctimonious peace he was looking for now.

He unlocked the front door and gave the knob a twist. His eyes weren't prepared for the tufts of fur like snow scattered across the linoleum-lined floor. He stood in the doorway as all the air was steadily ripped out of him. He stammered and stumbled inside, shutting the door behind him. His feet carried him along the furry trail. It was a surreal pathway of dismay rising into his eyes. Slowly, his feet scraped the floor, scuffing it as if it were layered in tar meant to slow him down. He made it into the kitchen, paused, and yelled out for his cat as tears began to well in his eyes. "Frisco!" He swallowed his heart which had risen like a geyser into his throat. He couldn't even tell if it was still beating. Dread had a firm grip on it. His vision blurred from the tears. There, he found the sullen truth of what he had hoped to avoid. Hypnotized, he wandered into a siren's song to find the signature of blood smeared on the walls of his bedroom. It was this truth he wanted to avoid. The truth that his mind already knew would be the conclusion to the sight that was before his eyes—those tufts of hair he saw when he opened the door.

He crumpled on the floor like a wadded piece of paper that had been tossed at a trash can only to miss. He felt the hot tears release fully, stinging his eyes harder, streaming down his face as rivers of misery. His nose opened their flood gates, running down. He gazed beyond the blood-spattered glass, through the salt haze of his eyes, to the fish in its pristine water. He screamed, "What do you want?" A wail of torment slipped through his lips. That cat had been his only comfort from all he'd been through, from deployment to his divorce, to his current state of mind. His vision continued to blur like an alcohol-fueled stupor, objects multiplied in the veil of emotions that flowed like a spring of torment.

His cries carried on when her voice, in its calm serenity, said from behind, "You were giving the cat more attention than me and you can actually hold me."

He quaked with rage and despair from the events replaying the past two days over and over, flooding his mind like a sea of liquid fire, burning everything within him. All the while, with the voice carrying on in such colloquial sweetness, so sweet that in fact it might as well have been aspartame luring out cancer, she said, "You went through all that effort to save me. We can be together forever. In fact, I think we both know that we belong together forever."

Rage helped him cling on to the world. He whipped around with a swing to find no one there, yet the voice persisted. "Don't be like that, Andrea. Don't you remember me? I remember you with your iron will and strong arms that I always imagined wrapping around me." She ended her words with a schoolgirl's giggle. His head began to swirl. He felt out of breath and began hyperventilating. Anxiety took over, grabbed onto him like a gorilla squeezing the consciousness out. He collapsed to the floor on his side.

The voice continued as the walls closed in on him. She said, "Don't worry we'll always be together. I chose you. Don't you remember when you were over at my pond throwing food? You said it was your second time away from the states."

His vision continued to narrow until all he saw was the sky-blue girl leaning over him, bending down, and kissing him forcefully. His jaw was locked by his own emotions with no way to speak as PTSD wrapped its tendrils around him with its kraken maw ready to devour him. He could only sit and listen to her as she flipped him onto his back. His fading mind understood how psychotic this was.

She said, "You were in Japan, and I wanted to go with you, I even listened to you every day until one day you were just gone."

Finally, he drifted off into the world of blackness, the stress triggered frames of the desert as guns blazed into hot winds blowing by, so many scenes of bullets whizzing by into friends, after what seemed like minutes he was rudely awakened by an extremely forceful pressure on his face. He felt what could only be claws dragging across his face like sheets of paper delicately cutting into his skin.

She said, "You know, it's rude to fall asleep when someone who loves you is talking to you."

He grimaced from a soreness radiating from the back of his head that seemed to be swimming in a warm sticky fluid, in his shock and blacking out she had to have been more forceful with him than he realized in the moment. His eyes popped open, almost ungluing themselves from being shut. The blur he saw before, the void he felt himself falling through into a time when he was in combat, had been wiped away now. As he felt himself not clothed at all, he stared at the sky-blue girl on top of him. However, he was also with her in the most intimate of ways with her smiling at him.

She reached down with her hand to caress his face. She said, "There you are, my love. I knew that if we made love that I could spur you back to life to share this beautiful moment where we were consummated as one."

Rage took over. Of all the things he had to suffer, now this thing was trying to make him love her by force. He shoved her hand away with a quick swipe by pushing her off him, though it was a rush of adrenaline and fire laced vitriol that didn't last very long. As he tried to get up, he noticed that there was more off about him, like all the lacerations on his arms, the basic struggle to even move enough to get to his knees. The attempt to sit upright was interrupted by a foot crashing down on his face. He fell back to the floor spitting out blood and a couple of teeth. His voice came through gurgles of blood and newfound pain pounding over his body. He demanded, "What do you want, you psychotic freak?" In a willful act of defiance, he tried to get up again, rolled on to his side to shakingly get up, only to have his hands swept out from underneath him sending his nose on a crash course with the hard floor, leaving another blood splotch.

She got down on her knees and cooed at him softly. "Just stop fighting and be with me forever . . . I don't understand your side of the energy. You fed me every day, you talked to me every day, and the way those rich brown eyes looked into my soul . . ." She paused briefly, gazing at Andrea, before continuing. ". . . I knew back when you were a soldier in a foreign land that we were meant to be, and no one else can have you, Andrea."

The fury wasn't enough of a steroid to lift him up off the floor anymore. His body was spent from whatever happened to him while he was off in the past, reliving a world he'd left behind, yet still managed to follow him for the rest of the time that he'd been alive. His brain ran at light speed, bouncing from place to place like a pinball in a machine that was headed for the high score, going through everything he had ever done up to that point and he knew he would remember meeting whatever this thing was.

With arms and legs shaking from trauma, he spat out another mouthful of blood, turned his head to one side to keep his face out of it, and forced out the words. "We never met while I toured in Japan. I used to be married and happy . . . I don't know who you are."

The sky-blue woman finally expressed a look of anger as her voice changed, and so didn't her reluctance to just beat around the bush. "You don't know me? You don't know me? You don't remember feeding koi fish at the pond? You don't remember giving me hope? You don't remember telling me all your stories while you looked off at the sunsets?"

Her soft cooing had officially turned into a molten magma rupture of rancid anger that came pouring out like a volcanic eruption. She continued her rant at Andrea, as he lay face down in a puddle of his own blood. "I knew all the way back then that we were meant to be together. I went through a lot to make sure we could be together forever, Andrea."

The pain became riddled with the anguish of the wounds mixing into the swirls of blood and madness that she was spouting; he didn't have a chance to examine his position in terms of anything before she started beating him. That was still a curious caveat to the situation. Could he get out of this or was this just one of those situations that, no matter how you tried to get to the best outcome possible, would end up like a rigged deck at a crooked casino? He moved his arms forward to be above his head.

She frothed at the mouth in a rabid rage that seemed to infect more of her brain.

He said, "What do you mean, you did so much?"

Her gaze was a grizzly bear waiting to swallow up unsuspecting salmon. "I memorized your name, your face, the way you talk, and I even altered the way your ex-wife's chemicals transmitted in her head. That's right. I did everything for you. I can control water, Andrea. And what are chemicals, but water and trace elements locked into a certain array of atoms? Your ex-wife? Laughable—as if she ever deserved you."

Her twisted giggle radiated off the walls in a sickening bass. "I've been nearby for a long time. I just needed you to decide you wanted me, which you did when you bought that run-of-the-mill goldfish. I know you were thinking of me, but now you're being so ungrateful even after we made love right here on the floor." It was this interlude where she began beating him again until he coughed up his own blood once more, the drops clinging to his uvula, causing him to gag. She was strong for such a petite thing; the looks truly were deceptive. Andrea couldn't make a sound from all the pain. Sound or not, wheels inside his brain began turning in a different way where it clicked, and he began to understand the level of psychopathy going on in something he didn't even know existed until now. He angled his head to see her. Her beautiful face had twisted into a deep-sea nightmare with tubular teeth jutting out, angry glowing coals for eyes. A rankled face with creases of a sea creature ready to unhinge its jaw and devour him down.

Andrea finally found his tongue. "What are you?" A simple question, really. But with her, nothing was simple.

"I am the water, and you are the fire. I will quench you and drown you with my love." She lifted his limp, frail, shaking body that had lost its strength from the continuous beating. She herself, at a certain intersection, had decided not to give up on him. She held him off the floor. He dangled in pain, like bait on a hook, ready for a deep dive into the waters below. He watched her unhinge that jaw that he suspected was going to do so, stretching impossibly wide. Her eyes sunk in with the remnant of the beautiful sky-blue girl disappearing as a thief in the night, standing as the monster she truly was, doing whatever it took to fulfill her obsession. Her mouth opened like a vortex as she sucked him down. The world faded for Andrea. And soon, those same emergency vehicles that had been down the street returned after no one had seen him at work.

Police rummaged through his property, trying to find answers to the blood stains and tufts of fur. An officer was stuck staring at an aquarium tank with two koi fish with opposing patterns. They were swimming around in a rather peculiar way. One was clearly trying to chase down the other, though the exact reason just couldn't be determined by the officer. Officer Cortez did his best to try to piece the clues together. But ultimately, this was going to sit on the shelf for a long time in an evidence locker that most definitely needed to be cleaned out, after all, he had other things he needed to tend to these days.

The god in yellow

I think it was the sudden flash of light, white phosphorus punching into the pupils blurring the sudden expansion of hot gas to the face, dissipating. I began watching nebulas swirl in a dense mix like ingredients in a soup that had just begun to cook. Maybe it was because I finally saw it for the thirty-seventh time in a row of everything rapidly moving into place, a time lapse of a puzzle where nothing has turned out right in any of the previous versions thrown before my eyes, no matter how I possibly stretched my arms to reach it. To twist the pieces around into place, things might make a more complete picture, where everything could finally interlock into peace and harmony. It was always pointless, limited interactions were a frigid slap to the face, it's just not what I really imagined. That wretched voice echoed like an atomic blast, a shockwave that always sucked the very breath out of my lungs.

"Choose your laws of physics." I always hated this part, it seemed trifling at best, picking a way for the universe to develop for all its interactions, only for it to come crumbling apart as a sandcastle getting washed away under the crush of a wave.

It always felt like a mad man's science experiment that would grow wildly out of control, a sea of flames reaching for the canopy of trees consuming everything within its voracious maw. My rattled tongue pushed out the words "Magic, alchemy, and a tinge of science." The question itself would just continue like an automated telephone line that hadn't received its input yet. My mind finally flowed as if it were a dam that had held back a shelf of water where it could finally be released, if I could interact with them a limited number of times. I was going to make sure that every interaction I carved into the stone face of this cycle meant something that couldn't be misinterpreted. It wasn't going to be like the last thirty-six cycles where they essentially blew themselves out of existence, where everything ended in obliteration fueled by supernovas of hatred and apathy. There would be no more madness running rampant through the stars infesting everything as a trans-dimensional cockroach scuttering from one star system to the next, gobbling up everything it got into its mandibles.

I had never known of a god referenced anywhere in any religion in all my years to wear a yellow robe on a dimly lit throne of alabaster, that devilish grin offering sickly sweet wafers as a form of communion. To be a thunderous hand clapping out waves that saturated reality with matter, precipitating reality into the fabric of being from the nothingness that stood before it as a permanently fixed substrate. I remember his words that still echo through the halls of my mind. They were like the hiss of a radiator cutting into the very essence of who you were, his very syllables hot enough to melt your eardrums as if they were candle wax set atop magma.

"Come with me, Mr. Rembrandt, my valued servant. I have something for you. A chance to be something more than you ever could have imagined in all your wildest dreams, for all that you've ever done." His words crackled as if they were the pops of a bonfire inside my brain, shooting glowing pieces of charcoal burning me in ways that I couldn't even begin to describe. It commanded authority with the heat and intensity of innumerable Jupiters colliding together. As he laid out a palm for me to take it, I looked back at my own body that was lying still on the concrete, with paramedics feverishly trying to resuscitate me, pumping me full of drugs, blood, CPR, and shock paddles trying to make the mobile EKG machine register a pulse that was hiding like a submarine in enemy waters.

I didn't know it at first from the rush of heat that managed to power through me, I thought it was adrenaline pumping through my system, a biological EpiPen injected straight from my own veins, making my skin flush. But as it turned out, I was in fact gunned down in the liquor store robbery. Officially treading into a place filled with mystique where my feet had never known, I had never taken any kind of stock in the world with its diverse religions, though at every turn I was learning about a new one every day at one point in my life. This, however, was irrefutable, he pulled back the hood to reveal his slicked tar hair. His eyes, though a familiar shade of blue, seemed to be filled to the brim of the cup they were in with ice cubes of madness that just gripped you in their stare. His eyes on their own could have made an appearance as a James Bond villain, and I would have accepted it, as I'm sure many others would have as well if they found themselves caught in their snare that could trap even a god. I grabbed his hand firmly with the same certainty as a guinea pig inside a lab for animal testing. His smile stretched like canvas getting ready for a paintbrush to stroke out the scenes clearly visible in his mind.

"Excellent!" The words evaporated off his tongue like hot water into the winter morning air, while everything shifted into a swirl blurring everything around us, a world of color washing down the drain into a pitch black illuminated by him with a singular dim light above himself on an alabaster throne. "You get to be god today—well I suppose you'll get to be god every day as long as you happen to be here in my domain." This was followed by a sharp laugh that churned my stomach as if I were still alive.

My tongue was caught like a hiker beneath a boulder on a trail never prepared, caught in a rockslide sloshing them down like water into a resting place. Yet still, I murmured, "How would I do that?"

The right hand patiently resting on the throne came up with the index finger like he wanted to accuse me of something. "Think of it like a game of twenty questions. Tell me your demands, and I'll make it so." As his mouth curved itself out into a smile moving like molasses in chilled air, little droplets of porcelain peeked through into an eventual ever-stretching myriad of white to pair with his throne in a matching set. "Do you think you can handle that?"

The lump in my throat that refused to be swallowed seemed to betray the stoicism that I was trying to broadcast to the situation at hand. This was a tremendous responsibility to ask of someone who had known nothing of leadership their entire lives. Yet, here I was, nodding and agreeing to something with a simple choked-out, "Yes," like a man in desperate need of car but didn't want the details of the paperwork to suddenly change his mind, a façade presented that had never been a description that matched who I was. I was passed over for a basic promotion at work to mid-level account manager at the bank because upper management didn't like my choice of ties, or I suppose there was the fact I refused to allow that place to rule my life. It was almost as if in some way there, at that little stretch of concrete and brick, they felt it was like a castle, and the manager, Cheryl, she practically viewed herself as the reincarnation of Queen Elizabeth. Despite what was going on around me as things shifted into being, I remembered that life almost nostalgically, I was always Joe and never Mr. Joseph Rembrandt.

The white throne with the one who sat upon it had vanished into the obscure inky black that surrounded me. I felt like perhaps it was just an odd happenstance of a dream that one would have on their deathbed, a bizarre hope of the things to come in the hereafter that I never wished for. Not quite like the flash of your entire story that I had been told so many times before would roll past your eyes like an unedited film showcasing all the ups and downs from start to its inevitable finish.

His voice erupted with a resounding boom out of the void into which he had disappeared. "Tell me, Mr. Rembrandt, how would you paint this universe? Oh yes, the pun was intentional, I already know there is no relation." He certainly maintained a special sense of humor, even though I could tell that it was in fact an attempt at it, it was more like nails being driven into your bones, rather than something that would make you laugh. With him no longer visible I felt the ability to speak easing back into my vocal cords, relaxed to the surroundings that were far less jarring than everything else I had been subjected to in however long a period had truly passed.

I said, "Well, I come from a world of science. Why don't we create a universe based around that?"

His voice groaned like high tensile steel under stress, the same kind of ominous sound that submariners face as they slowly sink too far into the murky waters of the ocean, all from a place I couldn't see. "I expected a little more originality, but then again I suppose we don't always brace the storm outside of our comforting little shells from the elements." The sound of his clapping hands ripped past me with a force that I had never experienced before in my life as it pushed away the bruises to my ego with the blow-by. Yet from that clap I watched the light and heat rip through the cosmos as well. The sight was purely awesome, such a raw display of beauty unfolding like an origami swan being undone to show you the fold lines. As I watched, gas and dust particles danced into shapes, creating stars, shaping wild glowing orange planets. Everything flowed in a fluid motion, water running over a precipice into the collecting pools, years passed by in minutes, planets cooled and bloomed with trees. Each one simultaneously in view of their habitable zones, wildlife rose from the depth of the waters when his voice rang through the dimensional plane.

"Now you must choose one of each, to start the trek toward betterment and advancement."

That curious statement grabbed my attention as my brain spun in a vapid state, which eventually spiraled out into confusion. "I thought life just naturally evolved on its own, and began like that, forgive my ignorance lord—is that the name I should call you?"

My words prompted thunderous laughter that reverberated through my being in tremors so profound it was as if he was in front of my face. "Goodness no. All life has a point of origin. I just made it, so you didn't have to create all the unintelligent ones. So, what is it going to be? Do you want to see humanity rise across the cosmos?"

He seemed to skip over my own question to propose two of his own. They seemed like genuine questions, but I could feel his eyes trained on me like the crosshairs of a scope equipped onto a sniper rifle. Even though I couldn't see them, I felt them cutting into me like hot obsidian through paper with their cynicism, almost as if I should have known better. Spurring my brain into action, the thoughts scrolled across their teleprompter in my mind, for all its faults, humanity had accomplished some rather astonishing feats in my own life let alone what it had hammered into the foundations of the world over the course of the centuries.

Thumping my tongue against the inside of my cheek repetitively, I nearly fell into a rolling ticker of my own thoughts. "Let's give humanity a chance to rise and show us what they can colonize across the fabric of this reality." Simultaneously, perception warped into 50 different planets that became a focal point, like a fly on the wall, seeing the kaleidoscope of life with its different fauna and plants reacting to human beings coming into fruition. Disorienting at first, it was LSD and liquor pumped directly into my eyes, providing a visual that both amazed and made the stomach wretch.

The voice I was getting used to steadied me as I struggled to deal with this newfound omnipresence. "You get a limited number of times to interact with your creations. You can make one thousand appearances work, right? No time limit, but when you leave, that time has passed, and you don't get it back." This was the first and only time that I had ever heard him mention anything regarding a limit for the things that I would be capable of doing, which struck me as odd, though he must have seen the gears gradually turning inside my mind, pondering the possible reasons I could have to hesitate upon his rule.

"Just like a father to his children, you aren't successful if they can't learn to walk on their own. You'll have to take the training wheels off and see if they continue down the path you set them upon or if they crash onto the ground." Words that, at this moment, resonated with me like a mentor speaking to their student imparting knowledge that could be only understood fully as you gained years of experience, as from my own personal life it certainly made a lot of sense, you can't just keep the training wheels on forever. So, consciousness developed, I laid down laws from the very beginning with them all, telling them to love one another as they loved themselves, stipulating not to murder, to go forth and do good deeds.

In hindsight, I realized that even though I had been very direct, they interpreted it however they wanted and applied the words in whatever way seemed to benefit them the most in current situations. I kept intervening and trying to show them better ways for them to prosper, and inevitably they met the time for them to go out and travel amongst the stars. But in all the things I had seen, the fundamental question hit me as I questioned aloud, "Just as I am here with you now, doing these things, where do they go when they die?"

In the ever-developing conversation, his disembodied voice replied, "For a time they know relaxation and ecstasy in a world, you can call it heaven if you wish, but ultimately reincarnate back in the mortal plane retaining their souls in new earthly bodies." It was this moment that jarred me in a peculiar way. I had begun to realize that there were rules to everything that were not exactly explained in the greatest of details, as I heard the collective percussions of colonized planets from galactic wars. Slowly everything warped into a galaxy-wide fire that was not a part of the multitude of suns that propagated life on these planets. Things dissipated into a silent scream of anguish that blew itself into the cosmos from my own mouth, seeing the very life I transplanted into existence blow away like a wisp of smoke. The stabbing pain rippled in my chest tormenting me in a way that I had never known, granting a new threshold of emotional pain, as everything slowly wrapped back into the black void that left me standing before the alabaster throne.

"My, my, weren't *they* met with a particularly cruel fate. It appears one can intervene as much as possible, and yet they will forget the words you spoke as if they never happened." His words were a cruel whip to the back that matched up with the similar magnitude of his face in terms of being charismatically handsome. The sharpness radiated down from the high cheekbones of his olive skin that may have been imparted due to his yellow robe, which poked outwards and around, past his proportioned face of a rounded chin with a small cleft. He said, "Well, you've certainly got many other times to go and make your creations continue on, to prosper, and figure out the mysteries of the universe you laid out. A pity . . . but their souls have not vanished like a phantom in the morning sunrise. We will start a new one and give them another shot at life. All hasn't been lost. Their souls can be recycled back into a new design where they can claim another shot at destiny."

On the surface of his words and expressions, watching him talk with his large slender hands, it seemed like a merciful statement as if they wouldn't be in perpetual torment with seemingly endless chances. A cosmic die that would perpetually fall in their favor to just start repeatedly with a new play, a new chance to pick up and change the tapestry of fate that wrapped around their necks like a noose from the hangman's gallows.

It was as if he was reaching out with an iron hand, eloquently speaking in a sturdy tone where he could understand my pain with what had just unfolded before my eyes, like a father using colloquial words of wisdom to apply salve to a battered heart. The dim light above him was unwavering. It seemed a little brighter, though maybe it was just the comparison from the void to here in a light that existed with seemingly no source. Even so, his tar-like hair seemed even darker than before, almost as if it had become slightly viscous, as if it had a coat of oil slathered on it, a perplexing sight to say the least. I would have admitted at the time that perhaps maybe it was all just because of the cosmic swirl of creation, madness, and destruction I had just witnessed. Though I couldn't really place my finger upon exactly what had changed, he seemed as though everything about him had a measure of power added to all facets of his being. It was unsettling. It also seemed to offer an unseen measure of reassurance; my mind couldn't really begin to decide which way the emotional compass should be pointing in relation to everything that just transpired.

The god in yellow sneered at me through his frigid eyes that gripped me in their carnivorous jaws. They weren't the eyes of a benevolent god reaching down to offer a blessing with his resulting query. "Shall we give them another chance?" It seemed to be an innocently poised question that trailed Plutonian ice up the curvature of my back. Something in the countenance of his eyes just struck me in a way that, while it temporarily stopped my brain from spiraling out of control, it also made me wonder did he really mean that?

While I was lost, just looking at him, my mouth slightly parted with my lips allowing the words, "Let's try again," to roll out in loosely tied syllables, while my chest was still palpitating in pain from the last round. So, I changed things with a new roll of the dice, setting up another universe with avian people where my vision fractured into the stained-glass view of omnipresence, guiding them ever so slightly and stepping in only when I thought my words would grant them the most guidance. To watch as a plague discovered on a distant planet at the edge of the star system spread out through the cosmos that, even though they had reached a tier 2 civilization according to the Kardashev scale, ripped through them like a cannonball into tissue paper.

This seemingly game of chance as to how things would turn out in terms of results, despite my intervention, landed me right back in front of the god in yellow for more commentary that felt as though my very heart was being grated against razor blades, whittling away my very soul. "My, my, good show, you really put your A-game out there, such a melancholy ending from their blissful ignorance, it cut the cords of their lives short while they didn't even realize the scissors were in their own hands, all because they thought they'd risen above the heights of their creator."

I was certain of it now. He changed every time I came back to this space. His eyes were brighter, almost glowing like LED lights, granting them a severity that would cripple you if you looked at him too long. His hair nearly made the top of his head fall off into an abyss, as though it was a repeat performance of Houdini's forgotten act, to mystify only me since no one else could see it. The light was, in fact, brighter, revealing more than just his alabaster throne, it was seated on something that the eyes couldn't quite focus on, something that the eyes just couldn't make sense of. Maybe it was because the light was still too dim, or maybe it was because, despite newfound abilities in the perception of time and everything in the material world, they simply lacked the components to process it.

It was a cycle that repeated, the one civilization that gave me the strongest sense of hope was number thirteen with the collage of species intermingled together like the fibers of a shirt. Nearing the end of tier three in the Kardashev scale, they used so much energy from stars that, at a certain point, the collapses and supernovas in star systems were eating galaxies by the super massive black holes that were being created, sucking them down into infinite spaghetti. They were trying to rip holes in the fabric of their reality, to reach out and touch the almighty that transplanted them into the world, a sin that would never be forgiven by the god in yellow for their insolence, it trying to reach out and touch him. Superfluous, flashy with their technology that could make extraordinary things look like magic, force field technology through artificial magnetic fields that looked like the way the Bifrost was described. They created hard light, hyper lightspeed travel, and nanotechnology that could repair any disease. They could manage to live six hundred years at a time with cybernetic enhancements. It was all so thrilling to watch them develop and go into the realms of the unknown with the things they crafted.

Then, by exhausting their resources, energy depleting into the memory of a dream that was never truly clear to begin with, they had created such a massive pull against expansion that the universe began collapsing. Shrinking by a multiplication factor that would require a quantum computer just to place it exactly with an exponent, until life was crushed in a gravitational pull that left them like rats on a sinking ship with no place to go. It was the cycle that filled me with the most ebullient joy, fathomless hope, yet it was also the cycle that gave me a taste of abject horror shoved right down my throat like a lead coated fist. This led to the inevitable meeting in the same room, met by the same god in yellow.

He said, "My, my, it would seem as though they simply meddled with forces beyond their scope of reasoning. A terrible fate nonetheless." His boisterous laughter would have shaken the universe had it not just collapsed, as it echoed from his alabaster throne, now surrounded with enough light to show the sphere of swirling sulfurous gas beneath it showcasing the souls screaming silently through the barrier. They clutched their heads, writhing with pain and anguish, drowning in pools of immeasurable madness swishing to and fro from the pressure of wails unheard.

His hair had turned into a jet-stained pyre that rose a foot above his head, burning as it did, defying what fires were intended to do. His eyes were long past sunken in, and resting within the gaunt face were two portals to the abyss with shimmering blue dots trained on me like the gun from the liquor store robbery. Just patiently waiting with glee for me to move a step out of line, with his hands almost skeletal as they rubbed up against an emaciated lip that housed teeth sharper than any sea of knives. There was an eagerness in his voice, it reminded me of some of the addicts I sometimes passed on the streets that begged for pocket change so they could get their next fix from the local dealer who knew that what he was doing broke so many moral codes, that he and Al Capone could have been business associates. The only problem, from where I stood, was despite the changes that had warped him so, I couldn't say he was sick. I couldn't say it was an addiction like a noose wrapping around his very soul.

Instead, he eagerly suggested, "Well, let us not keep them waiting on the chance for redemption." He practically licked his lips with a sharp pointed tongue against those ghostly remnants that rested upon his face.

It was clear to me that it was hunger that knew no bounds in its gluttonous appetite, seeking only the next meal of madness and chaos. I knew within the aching of my being that it wasn't for them to be brought into enlightenment from achieving the heights of society and evolving as a species. So instead, I locked my mouth shut to delay a kind of inevitable circumstance of him getting more of the tiny morsels, refusing to answer the questions, feeling his shift to disappointment and rage.

"Bold of you to assume you have a choice, boy," he bellowed, followed by the raking sounds of his hands against his alabaster throne. He unseated himself at a speed that I had only ever seen in superhero movies. Within half the blink of an eye, he was in my face with a breath hotter than anything that was ever thrown at me from any of the big bangs. His blade-shaped tongue almost tasting my ear, he said, "We shook on it . . . though if you'd rather . . . you could always join them."

My body revolted against me as the smell of putrid death swirled around my head, forced its way into my nose, filled my mouth with the taste of rot as it lathered the back of my throat on the way down. I couldn't help but nod.

The words slithered, a Komodo dragon salivating its bane at the prospect of prey. "Good choice, though it would be fitting for their creator to join them, that'd really be picking up a cross and wearing a crown of thorns." He mocked me in a fashion for a way I had never even believed, though I knew many who did, and I, myself, was not the praying type, though it did spur some temporary prayers inside of my head, at least or so I thought, as he cackled coarsely, as a machine of cruelty that had just officially come back online. "None of them can hear you in here. This is my domain, and they know better than to come where they aren't wanted, those young vain, prideful braggarts who claim property they didn't create." The words out of his mouth were filled in the fiery indignation of anger, aimed in such a way that I thought his syllables themselves would swallow me whole, a reticulated python just wrapping around my every nerve ending. A hand tapping against my face with its frozen flesh, patting me like an obedient dog that just finished its service training for the blind.

"That's a good boy, do as your master commands." I never knew that the darkness into which I vanished could be the comforting blanket wrapping around me to grant the illusion of peace.

The place that had grown on me; it became the fruiting mold that was now holding me together, so familiar with his voice telling me to choose things that to my knowledge were trivial at best, as it was now in the realms of my present thought, that it wouldn't matter what I chose, and so I too became infected with madness as it seeped in through my pores infecting my bloodstream. Choosing wild compositions, picking out spectacular arrays of physics, belief systems, and lower gods to rule over the mortals in the everyday worlds. The more I spun my wheels living out the true definition of insanity, the more I felt I had dived into the arctic embrace of each cycle as the world I had left drifted off by lightyears at a time. By cycle twenty-eight, I couldn't even remember what my mother had looked like or even her favorite lilac perfume that my aunts used to tease her about because of its old church lady quality. I could scarcely grab a hold of any moral lesson that I thought was engraved upon my heart so well, it was all so fleeting like a tiny wisp of vapor caught in a hurricane's gust, ripped into the expanse of the air.

In minutes or days, years, whatever time had passed up to here in cycle thirty-seven with the laws of physics being laid down as I described to the very letter, he placed gods on their thrones as I decreed, ruling mortals with their vain precepts. They had made it to the iron age, smithing amber-glowing swords when I felt the tingle radiate over me. I thought I was done feeling things since I saw countless nations rise and fall, so many universes exhaled out, dejected in their last breath.

It was then that I felt the skeletal hand dig into the back of my brain, ivory bone roots sinking in, reaching for water in the soil, static electricity turned into full shocks ripping into my chest, blowing away the very thoughts from my less than agile tongue. His skull burst forth from the depths outside the universe where we stood, fully aflame with black fire that illuminated itself against the black void. Crystalline blue laser beams locked onto my pneuma.

"Don't even think about it," he urged, but the rest of his words fell on deaf ears as another wave rallied in my chest, the suction began tugging harder than a diesel engine just beginning to warm up and switch gears.

Those skeletal daggers ripping through flesh and bone into the back of my brain diving deeper like white pillars into the ocean from Atlantean destruction, the swirl of miasma, that primordial mix of madness and anguish swirled inside of its sphere, tearing into me, ripping me open as a pack of hyenas in the safari. Stretching out my being, strands of light before a blackhole, time multiplied into a standstill that was incapable of being written down, pain flowed through every nerve ending as a tidal wave that was imperceptible to the human eye. Until that very moment, when everything just snapped and let loose with a sudden shock of lightning stabbing in my chest, the darkness swept away as fog took its place with the shapes of people frantically dancing within it. Beeps broke through the silence, voices clamoring that they had saved me from the arms of death and brought me back into the embrace of life.

A monotone rough voice said, "He's stable now, but he isn't out of the darkness yet."

I remember thinking that I didn't know if I agreed with that exact remark or even if what I was going through right now was reality, part of me wondered if I had finally broken and if I was just in the mixing globe of sulfur clouds that sat under his throne.

Eventually, I came to a uniform room filled with hospital equipment, where a nurse, her auburn hair, her gracious smile greeted me, she smiled so warmly at me with that beautiful tight-lipped smile, it seemed genuine albeit tinged with the remnants of her possibly bad day. "Oh good, you're awake, Mr. Rembrandt. I'm going to get the doctor so he can have a look at you. Other people are going to want to speak to you, too."

Was it all just a nightmare that had decided to place itself firmly upon my chest as I sat locked in the arms of death? Her voice was honey sweet, the syllables dripping with their sugar, but then again, I suppose anyone's voice besides his after all of that would seem like the most refined of candies. It was a pleasant thing to wake up to, a beautiful nurse who seemed like she cared, yet my mind couldn't help but continue to reflect on the murky experience that I went through as it kept wandering to the subject of a god in yellow. At certain moments it's as if the scenes flashed before my eyes with his staring back into mine, trying to burn a hole through everything that I am with their ice-blue fire that seemed as though it was capable of devouring anything in its path.

I am sure they assumed that perhaps I was having PTSD episodes of the robbery, the gunshot, being in a puddle of my own blood as I lay down on the concrete watching the world cascade away like grains of sand on the breeze. It was a reasonable assumption, and as such, they made referrals for me to speak with a therapist to help deal with the trauma of what had happened. I didn't know if I was capable now of really telling what ailed my mind.

Days came and days left, and my wife Louisa, my children, Samantha and Gregory, came to visit me. Eventually, I was able to go home from the hospital, where I would have episodes that my wife would always question. It really led me to question the nature of the world we live in and if we were on the same rails as every universe I had helped design as it careened into a ball of wreckage that plumed with madness. Eventually, since time seemed as fast as all the universes that I had created, I stopped by a church to sit and talk about gods and the nature of the universe on which I had become lost. Though I had never been one for it, a little bit of faith couldn't have done me any harm.

It was a church surrounded by trees on the side of a black asphalt road that had not seen any maintenance except for when it was originally laid down, almost as if God himself had planted it there in the place of the other trees that would have grown. Flakey eggshell paint greeted me as I stood outside of the door. The paint, however, was in much better condition than the black shutters made from aged vinyl that might have been around when Elvis could have been playing on the same material. The parking lot was just matted down dirt with flecks of cobblestone gravel. The little countryside church held its charms, oak pews with fresh lacquer on the inside of its walls that lined the way to a man with a priestly collar.

He greeted me with a warmth indicative of his calling from underneath his salt and pepper hair. "Well, hello, son. What brings you to church on this fine day?" His well-spoken tones and overall appearance took me aback a bit as in comparison I was a slightly overweight middle-aged guy that was lucky to have been with the woman he got in the first place.

I piped up, though you could say I was a bit nervous, since this was really the first time I had been in a church since being forced to go as a child.

I sauntered towards him and said, "Well, firstly do I call you father or . . . do you have a name?"

A chipper laugh greeted my question at first, which was then promptly followed up by, "You can call me Father McCarthy." His freshly baked warm cookie-smile illuminated his face as I walked up and shook his hand. His azure blue eyes had their own kind of light that made me feel at ease.

"Well, Father McCarthy, my name is Samuel. I came in today because I have had a lot on my mind since I got shot some time ago, and honestly, I experienced something that I just can't really explain."

He waved me on to follow him in a very laid back, easy demeanor, as he said, "Had a brush up with the divine, have you?"

I followed him back to his rectory at such a relaxed pace.

I responded, "Yeah, you could certainly say that. Although I'm not sure if what I must talk about is what others might bring to you." We passed through the front of the church heading off to right into a hall that contained a cherry mahogany door that maintained its mundane features.

"Oh, many people feel that way, Samuel, but I can assure you that nothing surprises me these days anymore." That charming priestly man opened the door and motioned for me to have a seat. "Why don't you tell me all about it? Hmm. Would you like a bit of tea or coffee or maybe some communion wine? I hear it helps loosen the lips a bit."

His giggle at his joke threw me off a little bit, but then again, anyone could have a sense of humor. I got seated in an antique wooden chair with slightly frayed wicker backing to it.

I said, "Uh no. I think I will be fine. So, tell me about God."

The priest got seated in his own chair which in comparison was starkly more comfortable looking since it appeared to be a rather high-dollar computer chair, it was something that didn't quite match with the rest of the flow of the room. As the rest of the room appeared to be in line with what I was seated in, from pictures of the last supper to bookshelves with crown molding, it was him and his computer chair that seemed to break the rigidity of the room as the words began to flow out of his mouth in a calm fashion.

"Well, God is kind, loving, and all-knowing. He gave us his son to atone for our sins, his ways are not our ways, and though we try, our wisdom collectively would only be a drop in the bucket the size of the universe compared to his." As the words left his well-kept face that could have stolen my wife if he had been in the dating scene, along with him being in much better shape from what I could tell while he adorned his priestly clothes, not only had he beaten me fair and square in the looks department, but he also stood about six inches taller than me.

Of course, I am only five foot ten, which sent a breeze of envy through my rather unfocused brain, so the next question that came out was unintentional. "What made you want to be a priest, of all things?"

He gave another light chuckle, and responded, "Oh, well, some of us are just called to do certain things. It's best if we don't spend too much time dwelling on the how or why. But I don't think that's exactly what you came here to ask." He must have been reading the other parts of my mind with a statement like that, deciphering the hieroglyphs of my body language, the look in my eye, or even the clothes I had on my back that day. Which caught my brain in its trap, to be so well adjusted, he must really have seen a lot of people to understand what it looks like when someone is troubled.

"I suppose you're right on that notion, I came here because I had an experience that defied all of my previously known knowledge, something that for the life of me, truly keeps me up at night since I died."

Despite my pause, he looked at me sincerely, and said, "Well, I'm listening, son. It sounds like you have a rather heavy weight on your shoulders, like the story of Atlas in a way, the Titan the Greeks believed held the cosmos on his shoulders."

It was something about him, the way he composed himself, his body language in relation to mine, maybe it was the melodic tones of his soothing voice that just made him like a sapper, just like that, the dam busted loose. I sat there for the next few hours conversing with him about everything that I had witnessed, though at the end of it, to my surprise, he wasn't horrified, mystified, or in any way turned from my tale.

He chimed in, "Well, he does sound like quite a frightening figure doesn't he? Almost sounds as though he gives Satan a run for his money in depravity and wicked nature." A sentiment that I could most definitely agree with.

I said, "So, Father, what do you think all of that means?"

He tapped his lower chin as he seemed to be lost in his own thoughts. "Well, my son, it would seem as though what I said back at the beginning of our conversation, about not getting lost, not dwelling on things, has come full circle as a self-fulfilling prophecy." This riddled me with a bit of confusion.

I asked, "How do you mean father?"

He slowly erected himself up from his chair. "Well, I would say that if you wish to reflect on the matter and how it relates to you, I think there could be some fruitful works to come from that, but otherwise I wouldn't get lost in it so to speak. As with anything if we find ourselves extremely focused on, it can drive us into insanity as our chauffeur."

Curiosity was looming inside of my skull, I didn't have nine lives to lose, still I pressed him further. "Well, I mean I can understand that, but I don't know. I guess I was looking for something just a little bit more concrete."

He hobbled over to his bookshelf lined with volumes in a fighting formation and began spanning it as though he was looking for something. "Well, my son, if you're looking for a spiritual diagnosis, I would do some hard searching in your heart to repair all the damage that you've done to yourself and to others, and then I would try my best to let the experience itself go, as it sounds as though you're beating yourself up over unintentional sins." He then carefully pulled a book from the shelf and brought it to me. "After all, I don't think it matters much anyway."

His statement caught me off guard, so much so that I tried to get a better look at the book he was holding as I got up from the chair. I locked eyes with him. The beating in my chest stopped as a familiar feeling of time standing still creeped in. Those warm summer sky eyes had turned into the arctic breeze of a stare I knew all too well. The wallpaper was a sulfurous shade of yellow, not like the eggshell neutral that I had walked in on.

Looking down from the eerie smile stretching across his face frame by frame, I noticed a book labeled *The King in Yellow* that started my heart again, as it began to feel like an engine redlining in a car that was barreling down a lost highway against the drag of wind. Face to face locked in a stare, I began to bolt, swiftly pumping my knees into my chest. As I turned away, the walls turned into that noxious yellow gas, the silent screams of faces morphing into the walls with the outlines of their faces that bubbled underneath the surface of the paint. Lurching against the tension of the paint, their arms outstretched for me, testing the stretch of the latex.

I rounded a corner into the hallway we came in through, down came the phantom arms successfully reaching out from the gas that I burst through as it spiraled in the wake of me breaking through. With ever-reaching ghastly limbs grabbing and making contact, grappling at every pass, the resistance grew until it was as if I was breaking through walls. On the edge of my heel, with ragged breaths from the adrenaline, almost outside the door, I felt the final grab that stopped me, hitting a camouflaged brick wall that just yanked me off my feet.

Looking back over my shoulder, it was him laughing at me. "You didn't think I'd be waiting? You didn't know I always had my eye on you, Sam? I love your creativity, even while you run away from destiny!"

As I pushed forward against his steel grasp, the adrenaline finally kicked in. I felt the back of my shirt tear where he had a hold. I tumbled out the front door and down the steps that led up to the door as I scrambled back up further away.

He came to the door at the bottom of the steps but went no further. "You can run, Sam, but time is on my side! I'll be waiting for you. After all, my ways aren't your ways, and my wisdom is like an ocean to your teardrop." His manic laughter rang in my ears as I felt the sun on the spot where my shirt had been torn in such a large strip. He wouldn't go past the steps from where he stood, which painted the obvious answer that, even though I had fallen out, he still tried to grab me in my fall. He shouted, "I'll be waiting Sam, we will meet again." His harsh cold words clung to the air filled with the fumes of the church, as it broke apart turning into dirt. Ghastly yellow vapors were carried off in a breeze. He and the church both disappeared with the wind.

I was petrified, stuck to the ground in one spot, as the whole process took place, nailed to the ground where I had landed on my side, where his eyes could burn into the fiber of my being one last time. Eventually I got up, dusted myself off, awash with so much anxiety, that I thought I was on the verge of having a stroke. Personally, I would have welcomed the alternative of being there with him in any kind of form. Cautiously, I made my way back to my car, where I stared at the spot that used to hold the church. It looked like the church had never been there, no building left standing as it jutted out from the trees that surrounded it. I stood next to the driver side car door of my reliable Toyota. I started up the engine, sat catching my breath for ten minutes, trying to get hold of myself with all the things that happened only for them to vanish out of this world, as if they had never even truly existed.

His face popped up every couple of miles in my peripheral vision, burning into me with his eyes, his mouse trap smile waiting from the tree line. It eventually reached a stopping point, like a big red sign posted for him to wait until the coast was clear. Finally, I pulled in the driveway of my old colonial home.

The sounds of hospital equipment beeped starkly in contrast with the stunned silence that sucked the life out of the room. It was as if the story held Gregory's heart pinned against a wall by a car.

Samuel coughed shortly before speaking again. He said, "My wife, your mother, always wanted to know about these things, Gregory. She has been gone now for what feels like ages, but that's why I don't want any priests. That's why I don't anticipate having any amount of peace when I venture off from this mortal coil. It's also why I'm in no hurry for them to unplug these machines that I know are helping keep me alive. It's not the last time he has shown up. He likes to pop in periodically to remind me that I'm just a fish in the bowl made with his ridiculous power of madness and chaos. He will be back for me. After all, nothing can be so mad as a creator repeating the same thing repeatedly, expecting different results."

Visitors

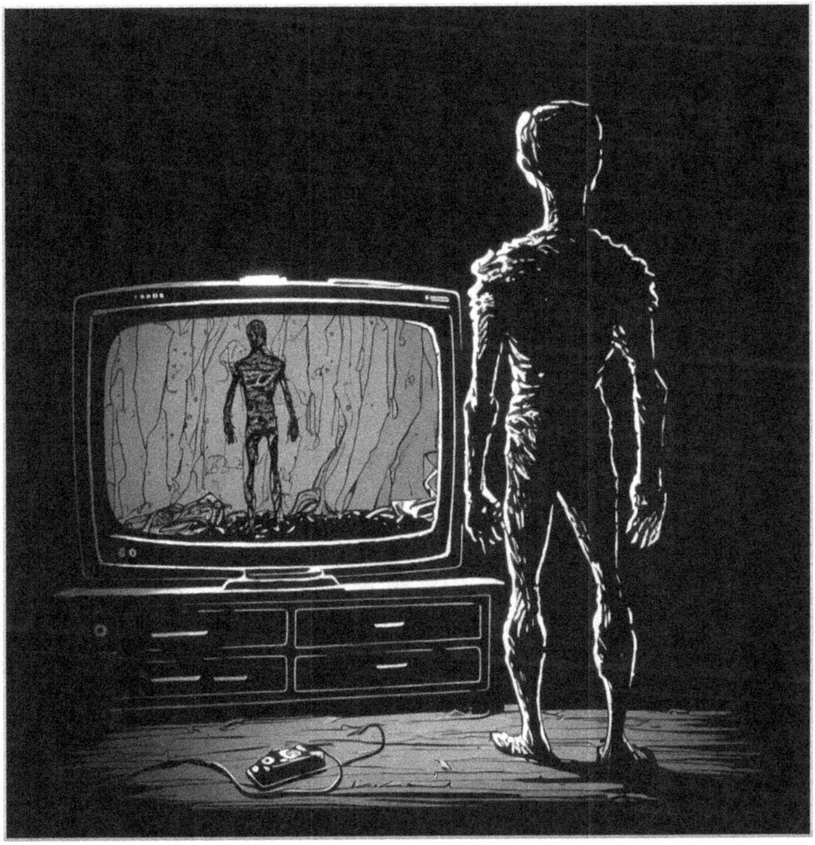

Television static roared like ocean waves slapping up against the shore in a continuous crash that created a hissing melody. Holding a certain harmony worked well for drowning out the world to Tucker's ears that grew excessively tired of the voices droning in with their constant insults. Speaking of rest, even if his eyes these days closed as often as a statue, a world where sleep just never seemed to permeate itself into his life anymore, there was still always something peaceful about the lull of white noise circulating the sound waves. Even right now he wasn't asleep. His eyes were closed, providing the scenic black to match up with the white noise. Just lying still could make the voices stop, which was just as good as getting the minute amount of sleep he could before the night terrors kicked in. They always came back like a bad acid trip you could have sworn you had walked out of only to find that everything around you was melting into a pot of primordial stew that would bubble away yet never be done. Perhaps it was the lack of sleep or the feeling of a constant dread that came with being awake that made him feel as though in all this chaos that was surrounding him, he had still come to a spot where he found himself.

Even at this very moment right now he was thinking in the third person, as if he was the narrator of his own story, sniffling and rubbing his nose, he finally stepped out of his own head long enough to utter the words, "Okay, that's about enough of that." Stretching out his arms, rising from the gravitational clutches of the bed he spent his nights on, getting up and out from underneath the covers, he almost tripped over himself leaving the comfort of that bed in a slightly messy motel room that looked like it hadn't seen a guest since circa nineteen-seventy. Up until the present day, he never even questioned if the walls were painted yellow or if they had originally been white, before they started making rules against smoking in motel rooms. Either way, it did not matter since the place didn't exactly reek of elegance and class. Not that he had the money to afford it any kind of way, as a guy that was getting by with odd jobs. Most of the town thought he lost his marbles not so long ago, when he started hearing and seeing things that they couldn't, which perhaps they were right about the subject, and maybe they were just as wrong as the Mayan prediction for the world to end in two-thousand-twelve.

If he was honest with himself, he wasn't sure if he felt any differently about the subject, since soon afterward he started getting prescribed medication. The meds themselves ultimately weren't too bad to take, though he did have the occasional side effect of needing to run to the bathroom. Of course, they didn't really make the voices of antagonization stop—or even lessen for the matter. It was a prattling noise filled with insults and secrets he didn't care to hear, stupid things like Mrs. Johnson had been cheating on her husband, or Dave Baker had a voodoo doll of his ex-wife in his car.

It was always some kind of trivial nonsense being whispered into his ears, as if he could actually go and do something about it, which in most cases was simply not the case at all. Not even within arm's reach of the sofa they had just installed into the room two weeks ago, where he would eat, pretending that he simply couldn't hear them echoing, gurgling, just like now coming through the radio. "Good morning, Keene, New Hampshire, and Tucker you little abomination. Didn't I tell you to see if that toaster you bought was waterproof?" Tucker's bloodshot eyes rolled around inside his skull from the side eye he was giving, like it was trying to polish back the shine in the mahogany color of his eyes that reminded people of tree rings out in the woods from past logging expeditions done by the logging company in order to keep the forests healthy and not overcrowded.

The white noise on the television that held the electronic blizzard which ran at all hours of the day, turned into the vision of a black robed figure in his sack cloth cloak, the contrast on the TV was in the sharpness of a pike, with a deep yellow that illuminated the room in the early morning. "He's still pretending like he can't hear us, like he thinks that will make us stop until we drag him down into the tar with us. Absolutely laughable, Tucker. You know you belong down here, where the river Styx circles our homes." Desiccated, sinewy fingers with patches of skin flaking off slowly raked across the television in a screech, sending an echo that felt as if that gray, malnourished hand was carving into his bones, writing in runes to possess him later. When one voice ended, another began like a chorus of acapella singers out of tune with one another, the toilet gurgled out, "Come on, Tucker. Aren't you tired of being awake yet? Isn't the idea of keeping your eyes open just unbearable? We're waiting for you; we just want to play." Then as often as it erupted out of the electric snow, though abrupt is how it occurred, so too is how it often ended with the speaking voices clearing out, and soon, the white static was all that was playing, much to his relief, though not because they terrified him anymore. Tucker, after a certain point, had grown extremely annoyed with them and their antics.

Taking in a deep elongated breath that he let out exasperatedly in a gust that could have blown out birthday cake candles, these interactions were never easy, and they never started speaking when other people were present. That's the time when they always seemed to be on their best behavior. Though people on either side of his run-down motel room would make complaints about the noise from the so-called TV shows, as he most definitely had zero control over the way they spoke or at what volume. It all played out in a way that made him question the validity of his own sanity, whether all of this was being played out by himself, either by him switching some kind of personality, or if they were auditory hallucinations, the possibility existed that these things were really after him, though of course it was slim. Chiming in like they did at such random intervals, if they were punching a timecard for whatever the case may be, the timing was always seemingly undeterminable. If it was something supernatural, he wasn't exactly sure what he did to anger extra-dimensional beings to start with. He began to rummage around in the miniature fridge for two-day-old pepperoni pizza that, in his opinion, was always better cold. He cracked open a Pepsi that he pulled out of the can drawer of the fridge and shut it again with his foot, halfway through with the two slices he folded it over into a homemade calzone as he called it.

He cracked his neck from one side to the other as the radio itself decided to crackle and pop with noise, suddenly coming alive with a premonition of the future for yet something Tucker would call another useless secret. "You've got a visitor, Tucker . . . She'd be fun to play with down in the fire." Trailing off into the dull continuous roar of a white noise hum that was cut through like a knife into paper by a sudden knock at his door that furrowed his brow with slight annoyance. Rising, still groggy from the never-ending insomnia, he got up, tiptoeing over to the door while he continued eating the pizza with disdain for the knocking coming at this time of day. He would recognize that black night hair anywhere as he eyed his peephole. "Predicting the future, are we now, Tucker?" He muttered to himself through a mouth full of half-chewed pizza. Slowly he turned the deadbolt until it clicked. He slid back his door to a crack just big enough through which to talk. Standing there in a bleach-stained black shirt and his boxers, his unkempt face with a five-day old beard, scraggly along his square jawline, he wouldn't be getting any modeling offers from Calvin Klein while looking like the homeless man he nearly was. The crimson lips with hazel eyes of the woman that had been knocking at his door heard the chain pop.

Tucker took the lead on the situation. "Serena! As beautiful as ever . . . now, what are you doing here?" he said in a tone that was sarcastic at best, though his unamused demeanor was deeply apparent to anyone visiting. Though he wasn't too rough with the situation, as her white veneered smile with those delicate cheekbones always did make her easy on the eyes.

She replied, "Well, Tucker, I needed to talk to you about some things, but you're just so hard to find these days."

Swallowing his next lump of food, he stood there not moving his hand toward the chain, simply refusing to unlock the door the rest of the way at that moment. "Oh yeah, well, lots of people want to talk to me about all kinds of things, so I'm gonna need you to be a little bit more specific, but you know it's almost like I might have it that way on purpose." His south New Hampshire accent was raspy from the absolute lack of sleep and still seemed like it could cut locks with certain enunciations. In contrast, her voice was delicate, like a phonograph playing smooth jazz on old vinyl.

She replied, "Well, I just, I've been going through some things, and I thought maybe you could help, you just seem like someone who would be more cut out for it, rather than the rest of the people in town."

His eyebrows raised in a way that would make you question exactly what was going through his mind in that moment. Would it be tear-filled laughter, or would it be something just as sharp as his accent? "Oh, is that so, Serena? You need my help?"

She began looking around entirely perplexed at the questions that were just asked her. She answered, "Well, I don't think I would have spent three days just trying to find you if I didn't need to talk to you about some, err, supernatural stuff."

Tucker sneered as he began to feel like maybe he was about to have a joke played on him that he just wasn't in on, which vexed him, the towns people haven't all been good to him in the turn of events that led up to where they were right now. "Listen, I'm not in the mood for this, Serena. I don't get enough sleep, I don't get enough food, honestly, I really don't get enough of anything that I used to. Actually, I'm lucky that I even have this run-down motel to come back to and try to sleep, along with that messed up Honda Civic out there." She tried to interject, but unfortunately, she couldn't rattle off any words before he cut her off. There just wasn't enough time on the clocks before he officially lost his patience for something he felt was going to be cruel. "Oh, for the love of Christ . . . leave me alone, lady. Remember, I'm just the town's resident crazy." He slammed the door in her face. The toilet gurgled like the belch from an ancient dragon, "At least you remember, Tucker."

Through the door in between them, he still heard the mumbling from the other side of the oak that had faced the parking lot for so many years, with so much paint on it that it made it more closely in line with a jaw breaker in terms of layers. It made the old piece of lumber nearly difficult to close. Tucker heard the words meandering through the door, slightly falling into his ears asking a question that he himself had never heard from anyone as long as his predicament had been going on.

"Is there someone else in there with you, Tucker?"

A sentence that made him fumble with the door out of shock, he had temporarily lost control of his senses and motor function. This was astounding. No one in all the time of him suffering through these things had ever even remotely heard one of their voices, let alone asked about them. Finding how to use his hands as rapidly as he could, he cranked down the handle, ripping back the door for it to get caught on the chain. Swiftly he shut it back before undoing it, then opening the door again, as he saw her strolling away. If he'd been a little less quick, he would have missed her entirely. He shouted, "What do you mean, 'is someone else in here?' Did you hear that?" His voice was poised like the curiosity of a cat that had finally become serious in its pursuit. Her feet stopped as though she had just landed up against a phantom wall that had materialized for the briefest of moments.

Tucker continued staring down the briefest of concrete pathways with a look of befuddlement, leaving his face contorted, his eyebrows sunken, and his mouth slightly agape.

She twirled around to face him. "I don't know who couldn't have heard that. It was kind of loud, Tucker."

He had thoroughly searched his brain for any memory from the moment he heard her ask that question, unable to find any other time in which he could recall that someone else had heard any of the voices. In fact, the black label of schizophrenia remained firmly mounted over the mantle in his brain. Squinting, lost in skepticism like the sun was shining directly in his eyes, he moved his head in a rolling motion and uttered, "Come in." Her extreme promenade was met with him enthusiastically closing the door behind her. He licked his lips, feeling the question on the tip of the same tongue he used to wet them, he un-furrowed his brow into a slightly less intense scrunched up expression. "So, what kind of a problem are we talking about here?"

Her eyes scanned the disaster of a place that he called home for the time being with disgust that couldn't be repelled from her face.

Tucker rolled his eyes. "Listen, I stopped caring, okay? Just be happy that it isn't Tuesday and I'm not having my alone time. Wait a minute. It *is* Tuesday. You'd better make this real good. Today is a *me* day, and as bad as things are, I don't like to miss those."

Tucker shook his head, walked back over and plopped down on the couch, where he took another bite out of the old pizza, finally finishing it off as he chewed. She also refused to step any further into the abode. "Well, out with it."

Finally finding her tongue after some moments had passed from her soaking in the grandeur of near-homeless living that Tucker had found himself in, she asked, "What is that smell?"

Swallowing that last bit of pizza at the tail end of her question, without skipping a beat, the words rolled off his tongue like melting butter in a hot skillet. "Well, I'm pretty sure it's stale pizza and whatever is growing in the walls, but *I* call it depression, so, the next question?"

The TV at that moment decided to roar to life on its own, popping up on the screen with a silent rerun of Wheel of Fortune where the host had been replaced with the dark-robed figure.

The very small chain of events that found themselves playing out on the TV caught her eye for more than a few moments when she asked, "Why do you stay here, Tucker? Can't you just leave, and then these things will leave you alone?"

This left Tucker slowly blinking at first, slowly thumbing his tongue against his lower lip, with both eyebrows raised. "Didn't you come here to ask for a favor or something like that? What's with the damn history lesson you want me to give you?"

Before she could return fire with her words, he spat out the answer she was looking for in the first place. "No, it doesn't work like that. They tend to go wherever I go—usually *places* are haunted, not *people*. I guess I got unlucky in that way."

Shuffling her feet as she grew a little uncomfortable from standing, she said, "I don't know, Tucker. It doesn't seem like so long ago that people wanted to be like you, and they actually kinda envied you."

Tucker's mouth dropped slightly ajar as he licked his top teeth from the emotional kick in the groin. He didn't need to be reminded of a life that vanished the moment he became so wonderfully endowed with his new guests that hung around longer than they were ever welcome. "Listen, the Boston Red Sox once upon a time won the World Series. But you know things change. So, are you here to judge me or, you know, do you wanna get to that other thing? You know the thing you supposedly looked for three days for me for."

The alarm clock radio started scanning radio stations in succession, with his favorite radio announcer's voice popping up on the air to come and bust his chops in some new profound way. "It's eleven a.m, Keene, and it appears we have a development in a new breaking story that Selena is concerned about Tucker."

Selena's eyes darted over to the radio, though she had heard the voice through the door. She never imagined that it was quite like this.

Tucker, however, interjected. "Ignore it. They know that you know. It's not going to stop just because you walked in here. It's better if you just ask whatever it is that you have on your mind and be done with it." The electronics shut off in sync, returning to their state of static that he enjoyed so much in comparison to the alternative.

Her eyes wandered back over to Tucker. "Well, I swear, I don't know how you live like this, but my nephew has been having a lot of nightmares, and lately he's been waking up with scratches all over him, sometimes he has bruises, even cuts. He's only nine and he has these bags under his eyes like they're trying to board a flight for Mexico."

Tucker raised his right hand and began rubbing his index finger on the very bottom of his chin, as if he had been transported miles away deep into thought. He had theories he wanted to test in relation to the guests that seemed to be sharing his life uninvited. Without question, this was an odd occurrence that they would have even revealed themselves to her to begin with, nevertheless he had other questions that needed to find their way to the answers.

"I've got my own questions, Serena. You just came in here and experienced some demonic activity, and yeah, maybe you're a little off put, but you're standing here taking it like a champ. So, either this is one of the most important things on the face of the earth to you, or there's something you're not telling me." Dead space reverberated off the walls as the two looked at each other for what seemed like hours, stuck in a stalemate where her lips didn't even try to move into a position where her tongue could begin to defend anything that she may have done once upon a time. "Got it, understood, a little of Column A and a little of Column B. That's fine. I get it. Maybe you messed around with a Ouija board and got a little bit more communication than you really hoped for when you were sixteen. Or, maybe, you're a horror fanatic and you're desensitized. I suppose you could have messed around with some magic in a phase you were going through and there were consequences you didn't count on."

It was at these words her eyes shied away with an unspoken shame. Though she had never said a word, her body language was putting on more of a speech than if she had prepared something ahead of time for the president himself to appear at a press conference on why the USA had invaded a country that just so happened to have an extremely large oil supply.

It was an exchange that, as her eyes moved, dragged out an exasperated sigh from Tucker. He rubbed the back of his head, now having a much firmer answer to go on than bad things happen to good people for no reason. "Fine, tell me where to be and I'll see what's up. But I think we need to talk a little bit beforehand."

Reluctance gripped her tongue and wouldn't let go. She fought against herself to even get out the words. It was a struggle that was also broadcast into the room rather well. "Okay, Tucker. I'm going to need you to meet me uptown. Go under Highway Nine and follow Walpole Road until you just get out of Keene. Our place will be on the right. It's the driveway right past the limit sign. You can't miss it. And Tucker? Please take a shower."

Tucker offered his sarcastic smile as a tribute to what she had to say. He was blatantly aware of the state he was in when she arrived. It was her fault for showing up so early in the day.

Serena turned on her heels towards the door, pulling it open to crisp air as it poured in.

"I'll be there, Serena. But just remember, I expect a talk before we do anything," he said. A statement that wasn't met with a whole lot of charisma, gusto, or, for that matter, any kind of hope.

Instead, he was met with a somber, "Of course."

He closed the door behind her and began getting ready for whatever kind of excursion he was in for.

The radio beamed to life as the deadbolt turned back into the locked position. "In breaking news, Keene, Tucker has got himself an adventure. One filled with mystique. Can he pull a rabbit out of his hat, or will he fail? Only time can tell, but if we know Tucker, he'll probably fail just like he does at everything."

He rolled his eyes as he picked out the only clean clothes he had left, a white button-up shirt in the double XL category and jeans that hugged him in a way that always made his underwear feel as though it was trying to bury itself in his backside. Unfortunately, there would be no underwear today since he was in dire need of going to the laundromat. Pulling a pair of socks out of the dresser, Tucker had collected his change of clothes, soon finding himself in the shower. He even took a disposable razor to his face.

The toilet gurgled out, "My, don't you clean up nice, Tucker. I can't wait to have your pretty face down here in hell."

Tucker gave a casual eye roll in the mirror, him being dressed up, his high cheekbones unhindered by filth or the beard that he had been letting grow, his curly hair puffed out into an afro, his square jaw lined up in such a way that he still could have been a lady killer if he had the resources. Putting on his elegant deodorant called Old Spice, he tucked his shirt in to see that he was still in shape, which was never hard for the five-foot-eleven guy with luck so bad that even death said, no, I'll let this slide, out of the purest sympathy.

Entering back into the main area of the motel room, Tucker made his way over to the old Nikes by the bed he rarely slept in. He slid them onto his feet. The shoes, with their faded blue and orange tie dye color pattern, had been a gift from so long ago that he always felt the need to stitch up with super glue. His keys were easily found on the nightstand by the radio alarm clock that could never keep its mouth shut. Double checking his wallet for the key card since it was really the only modern feature to this place, he made his way out the door and into the afternoon sunlight shining through the trees that stood so close to the motel. His eyes quickly landed on the 1977 Honda Civic that, for a while, acted as his home. He hated having to manually unlock the door, but things being as they were, it wasn't as if he was going to be headed out to get a new car anytime soon. He would have to win the lottery first or be treated a little more fairly from people for his perceived mental illness. Both of those things were extremely unlikely to happen. People seemed to be stuck in a magnet tar pit trap of stigma, that, hey, since you have this, we no longer consider you to be one of the functioning members of society. We just tolerate you giving the impression of morality.

Popping open the door, he settled into the driver seat that, at this point, maintained an imprint of his backside, which funnily enough, hadn't become uncomfortable yet. It wasn't quite worn down into the metal supports of the seat, but it was working its way there. Pushing the key into the ignition, he gave it a twist. The car had been the most reliable thing in his life—aside from the voices that pop up simply to torment him when no one else was around, which made it all the stranger that they had put themselves in the position to be heard by her outside the door. This, however, was not the time to be sitting here pondering things as he threw it into gear to begin his journey. The radio crackled to life all on its own, as he anticipated it would. They never let him get far before he was being followed like a woman in the shady part of town, not to torment him, but whispering secrets about the people he passed. Apparently, Mr. Hutchinson was cheating on his taxes, Laura Kroger was out running around on her old man again, and he wasn't the father of two of their kids. These secrets didn't do any kind of favor for him. What was he supposed to do with the fact that old Mrs. Hurley secretly resented her daughter for the fact that she moved away from town to be closer to her husband's family, leaving her alone with an abusive man who finally passed away two years ago?

It was always a bunch of information that should have been incoherent nonsense at best, but on the rare occasion that he had to confirm the secrets being presented to him, it ended in a disaster where people denied that they were doing those things, and pointed to a diagnosis to say he was crazy. This always left him in the position of feeling like he loved and hated people at the same time. He loved them because at the end of the day everyone was only human, but in stark contrast, he hated the things they did. His thoughts of everything melding together into a Damascus plate of thought which finally got interrupted by the radio chatter for a different kind of secret.

"Oh my, isn't it interesting that Serena Hensley is so fair, yet can never find someone who loves her?"

Usually, these kinds of things only popped up when he was in a certain range. Yet he was stuck at the light near the highway intersection, a few minutes from her house.

He listened closely to what the demonic radio host had to say. "Oh, did we finally grab your attention, Tucker? It's about time you started listening for a change. That girl is rife with magic leaking from her every pore. You think *we* have secrets? It's nothing in comparison to the one that she is keeping from you." The demonic chitter of laughter radiated through the speakers. He would have reached for the dial to turn it down, but it wouldn't have done any good. Besides, it was the last of the demonic chatter before he finally reached her house just outside of town.

Tucker killed the engine to the ragged-out Civic. He swept himself out of the car in a rather seamless fashion. Looking at the place, his finger couldn't quite poke itself into the reason that it would appear so insidious from the roadside or driveway. It wasn't terribly large as it lay surrounded by hemlock and silver maple. He slammed the car door and began his ascent up the driveway toward the colonial-style house painted sky blue. He knocked on the door and waited a minute or two before preparing to knock again on the solid wood door with its cherry red stain. The door pulled back away from his hand.

Serena greeted him. "Oh, Tucker. You're here. I didn't know if you would show up or not."

Tucker grumbled, "Yeah, you didn't know if I would show up or not. Are you ready for the conversation now, or are we just going to stand here and pretend like you didn't believe that I would show up?"

Serena waved him in. "You cleaned up nicely, Tucker," she said with a giggle, an obvious attempt at flirting.

"Uh huh, Serena. I'll cycle back to that in a minute, but the kinds of things you described are signs of demonic activity. We really need to talk about this." His words echoed off the foyer, as the house began to groan like it was settling a little more into the ground. His gaze wandered over the modern interior that didn't accurately reflect the same energy as the outside of the house in terms of style and décor. The living room was filled with modern furnishings and the kitchen had marble countertops with a garbage disposal in the sink. Things were posed in a way that looked nice, though the house kept creaking like it was trying to sink into the abyss. Appearances could often be deceiving though, there were many books in the world where the covers didn't accurately reflect the true story of what was going on inside the pages where people would get lost if they ever looked beyond what the surface had to say. The garbage disposal clicked on and off a few times by itself. Tucker said, "No, Serena, this has nothing to do with your cousin. What did *you* do?"

She stopped in the kitchen like a gyroscope just suddenly coming to a halt. "Tucker, I don't think it matters what I did or didn't do."

Tucker stopped her. "I am going to need you to roll that back just a little bit. It matters a whole lot what you did or didn't do. You lured me over here with a lie. You claimed your nephew was having problems, and I get here to your place and it's like the legions of hell are trying to storm the walls, so I'm going to need just a little bit of transparency."

Before she could respond to Tucker's annoyance, the drywall cracked in the kitchen where they were standing. "Tucker, listen, we all make mistakes, okay? We try to go after the things we want, then the next thing you know, everything is just blown out of the water like a fish on the beach gasping for air. I made mistakes. Why should we have to pay for them forever?"

Tucker cocked his head as the timber inside the walls cracked. "What *is* this thing? No, you listen Serena. We didn't work out. It's fine, things happened, we got divorced, you got a different house. You apparently have a demon that is actively exerting a pressure on this place right now that can royally screw us both to hell. I need you to stay focused and tell me what you did. I can't resolve this if I don't know." With those words, the house itself shifted as more drywall cracked and the nice hardwood floor buckled in places.

Serena couldn't look him in the eye as she stood there in her flowing sundress, her beautiful face with its tanned tones looking dejected and morose. She said, "I just wanted us to be together forever, Tucker. You never noticed me, Tucker." The floor appeared to be getting sticky with globs of tar that pooled as she spoke. "You wouldn't even bat an eyelash at me in high school. So, a friend of mine told me about a book of magic." The energy efficient windows began to rattle, the black tar substance started to leak from cracks in the drywall. "I just wanted a world with you, so I used a love spell, and I've used so many other spells since then. It just made everything so easy."

Tucker's eyes shot wide open, in the midst of a house that was being destroyed by demonic interference into the physical world. Ordinarily it wouldn't have elicited this kind of reaction from him—even in the most extreme of cases. He had seen these filthy tar monsters rise out of the depths before, with the face of jealousy, because they wanted him more. Maybe it was protection or because they wanted to eat his intangible parts for lunch. It was really anyone's guess. "Serena, my god," he said, as he looked down at his right hand that glowed with a tetragrammaton. "I'll clean this up, I will." A brief pause met him before he uttered the next word that didn't mean anything in relation to the things that they had just been discussing. "Akal." For a moment, all the interactions of demonic activity paused.

Unfortunately, the moment didn't last long. Tucker moved her behind the sink in the kitchen island. He ordered, "Get down and don't look." She obeyed as a sickly bubbling tar monster collected nearby. A screech from its emaciated mouth full of jagged needle teeth shattered a couple of windows. Its rage boiled over at Tucker. It charged at him, getting so close, it could have taken his nose off with a bite. But the claws that held it dragged it down with a sucking noise. Embers floated from a portal in the floor. The stench of rotten eggs flooded the house. The creature screamed and writhed, trying to break free from the claws sinking into it, pulling it asunder. Eventually the show was over. The screams fell silent. Little bits of ash were strewn about the house. The tar had vanished. Unfortunately, the damage to other things remained. It wasn't likely they were going to get the demons to pay reparations for the damage they caused. The glowing tetragrammaton disappeared.

As Tucker began to leave, Serena asked, "So, that's it? It's over? Can we go back to our normal lives now?"

Tucker stopped in his tracks. He replied, "It's over, Serena. It's done. The mess you made is back where it belongs."

She rose from her knees and approached him. "So, can we be together again?"

Tucker let loose a short laugh before getting serious. "Serena, for all I know right now, you're the one who inadvertently cursed me with this. So, no, we're not getting back together. You did something heinous when you cast that love spell."

As he walked out, Serena followed behind, begging and pleading for him to stay. He was the only thing that she ever truly wanted. Things just got so twisted up because she was so used to an easy road.

Now, as he neared his car, he turned around to face her for what might be one of the last times. "Listen, I'm tired. I really am. Apparently, I have a curse that devours the darkness out of others with a darkness that follows me. But this is the last sin of yours I'm eating. I've already consumed too many of them to begin with."

As Serena stood dumbfounded, Tucker crawled inside the comfortable seat of his Honda Civic. He started it up and drove down the road to the motel that he called home.

During the ride back, the radio, naturally, decided to come to life with more of its usual commentary. It spoke of the things people were going through from the weight of their sins. Sins that trickled through the ether, to a place where they could spit it back into Tucker's ears. Mr. Jones was running a front for organized crime with a chain of stores that sold mattresses. Mrs. Hinkley was deep in the realms of her severe gambling addiction. Doctor Richardson passed out prescriptions to opioid addicts for the kickback from the pharmacy. With the radio popping and crackling, it seemed this would be the place he would spend the residency of his life now, a supernatural pariah that the whole world would call insane and try to wash away with various medications. It wasn't all bad, though. He'd be able to help some people with the things he was capable of. And maybe all the secrets weren't useless after all, especially since here he finally gained some clarity about his situation. As he parked in front of the motel, the radio, with its special host, popped out, "Told you she had one hell of a secret, Tucker."

Dedication

Most importantly to me, you may believe in anything you wish, but I have to thank God for all of the time that I have had here in order to complete this and make sure that it got out into circulation so that other people can see that they don't have to let the darkness of their lives just eat away at them, they can do something positive with it in this world.

I would like to thank all the people in my life that have ever encouraged me to write a book, from my now deceased mother to my still living grandfather that I fervently denied that I would ever do for years at a time. It is long overdue that you get your shout out, you know who you are, be proud that you helped push me down this road.

My last but not least thank you goes out to all that have purchased and read the book, you are first on my list of people to thank, as without you this book doesn't exist out in circulation.

Peace be upon you all and I look forward to adding another book to your shelf in the future after this one.

About Steven Skibicki

Steven Skibicki is a 31-year-old Messianic Hebrew man from New Hampshire. He has been writing since the age of twelve. A staunch mental-health advocate, he has been diagnosed bipolar and is dealing with PTSD, but he's chosen a different way forward. He lives in South Texas near the gulf coast.

If you ever find yourself on the Strange Hwy—don't turn around. Don't panic. Just. Keep. Going. You never know what you'll find.

You'll see magic at the fingertips of an autistic young man; a teen girl's afternoon, lifetime of loss; a winged man, an angel? Demon—? Mother's recognition, peace to daughter; Danny's death, stifled secrets; black man's music, guitar transforms boy; dead brother, open confession; first love, supernatural? —family becomes whole!

You can exit the Strange Hwy, and come back any time you want.

See, now you know the way in, don't be a stranger.

Fresh Ink Group
FreshInkGroup.com

Comes this Time to Float
19
Short Stories
by
Stephen Geez

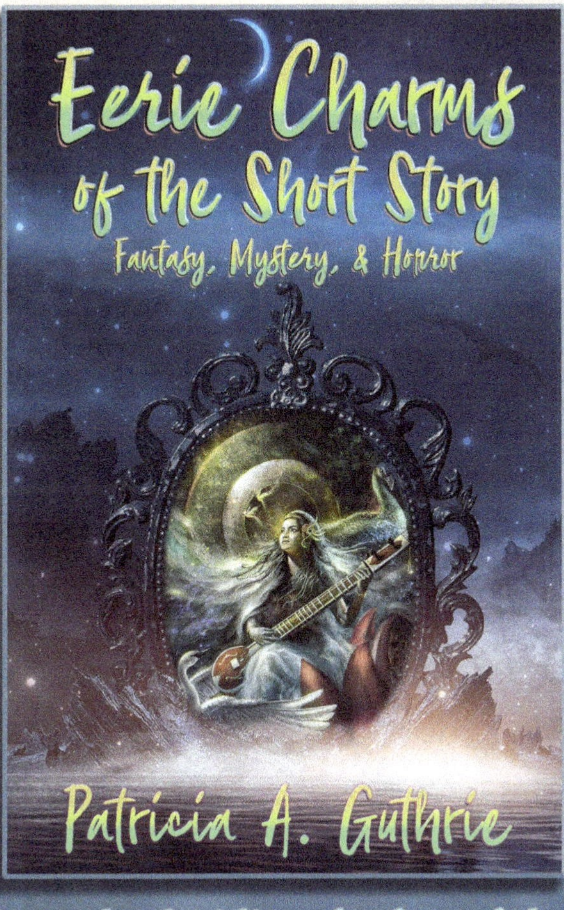
Eerie Charms
of the Short Story
Fantasy, Mystery, & Horror
Patricia A. Guthrie

www.ingramcontent.com/pod-product-compliance
Lightning Source LLC
Chambersburg PA
CBHW060550230426
43670CB00011B/1758
9781958922019